Spirited

Spirited

Living Between Two Worlds –
A Top Psychic Medium's Extraordinary Story

Tony Stockwell

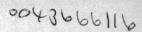

HODDER
MOBIUS

First published in Great Britain in 2004 by Hodder and Stoughton
A division of Hodder Headline
This paperback edition published in 2005

A Mobius paperback

2

A CIP catalogue record for this title is available from the British Library

ISBN 0340833548

Typeset in Sabon by Hewer Text UK Ltd, Edinburgh
Printed and bound by Mackays of Chatham plc, Chatham, Kent

Hodder Headline's policy is to use papers that are natural, renewable
and recyclable products and made from wood grown in sustainable forests.
The logging and manufacturing processes are expected to conform to
the environmental regulations of the country of origin

Hodder and Stoughton Ltd
A division of Hodder Headline
338 Euston Road
London NW1 3BH

To my parents Pat & Keith
For their love and constant support

My sister Lorraine
For believing in me

And most of all for Stuart
My best friend and companion
Who has shared my dreams and given them wings

In the next world

My grandparents; Kath, Bert and Betty
And Aunt Grace who made me strong

Those who have chosen to work alongside me
Zintar & Star

Acknowledgements

Thanks and love to all those who have helped me on my journey and belived in me: Mrs Payne, Canvey Island Spiritualist Church, Joan Barham, Marcia Ford, Hilary and Craig Goldman and all at IPM, Colin Fry, Vivian Foster, and Barbara and Janet.

Contents

Introduction

I believe everybody is psychic. We all use hunches and draw upon intuition to guide us when we are making difficult decisions or wanting to change direction in life. The extent to which we remain blessed with psychic abilities depends on whether we continue to draw upon this talent.

I believe I was born to be a psychic medium – that this was my destiny, and why I was granted the blessing of so many extraordinary experiences of the paranormal from childhood onwards.

From the moment I first realised that life is eternal and that it is possible to see, hear and speak to the dead, I was determined to embark upon the course of becoming a medium, and I have never looked back. I *love* my work and I am thrilled to have this opportunity to relate my experiences and to answer the kind of questions I am asked almost on a daily basis.

'What happens to us when we die?'

'What happens to animals when they die?'

'How can spirits communicate with us?'

'What is a ghost and what is a poltergeist?'

'Do evil spirits exist?'

'Is there a good way to die?'

'How can we prepare ourselves for death?'

The answers to these questions which, sooner or later, haunt us all, will be found in the pages of this book. But let me begin by explaining the work of a medium.

A medium's role is to offer evidence to the living that our spirit and our human personality survive after death. Mediums usually communicate through seeing, feeling and hearing the spirits that gather around them, and what results from this is often demonstrated in a 'one-to-one sitting' or public demonstration. A medium is usually able to give a description of the spirit and provide details of how they passed on, along with other personal information and messages that confirm their identity.

All mediums are psychic, but not all psychics are mediums. Psychics are very sensitive to energies that emanate from their surroundings, and they are also able to tune into people's auras – the distinctive air or quality that is characteristic of an individual. From these, they access information about the person's physical, mental, emotional and spiritual state, and can offer advice and guidance about problems or when the person is in doubt about the best course of action to take.

I feel I have been blessed. Never having felt the need to attach myself to any one particular faith or set of religious beliefs, I have had the freedom to study and take elements from different religions. I believe in the world of spirit and I have had many personal experiences that have shown me that our loved ones live on and sometimes wish to communicate with us. I also believe in reincarnation and have been granted several glimpses – visions – of my former lives. Eternity is not something that begins after we are dead, it is going on all the time. We are living in it right now.

I also believe in the law of karma – natural law – which means that I accept that how we choose to live in any one lifetime determines the circumstances that we are born into next time round. In simple terms, 'good' behaviour reaps one set of circumstances, 'bad' behaviour another. But I do not see karma, the sum of a human being's actions carried forward from one life to the next and resulting in an improved or worsened state, as an act of Divine Will, retribution or recompense. It simply means that each lifetime presents us with opportunities that enable us, if we rise to the challenge, to come closer to achieving our full potential – and happiness. If, however, we avoid what we need to learn, or run away from the opportunity to deal with a particular set of circumstances or a problem, these will go on re-presenting themselves, life after life, until we do face up to them. There is, in other words, no escape from karma! Any one lifetime, it seems to me, is rather like a board game in which we can go several steps forward or several steps back, but practice makes perfect!

I believe that we are all born intuitive, and that if we remain open, able to give expression to our emotions and sufficiently sensitive to feel for others, then we can all connect with the spirits around us.

Despite our natural ability to do this, however, only a few people feel inspired to take this particular path, and those that do discover that the work of a psychic medium requires a life of quiet reflection and a special kind of listening and devotion. 'What do you want, Spirit? What can I do for you?' becomes the order of the day. Yet, although a life of service is required, this is not a burden. We are blessed with the knowledge that the work we are doing is for the greater good; it is so rewarding to put those in need in touch with their loved ones, and to realise that this is a life-enhancing and belief-changing experience for so many.

The first requirement for becoming a psychic medium is the willingness to respond to the 'calling', that quiet voice within, and then to embark upon a vocation to bring the knowledge that there is life after death to others.

My spiritual journey began when I was sixteen. I still have much to learn and far to go, but however many days and nights I have left in this lifetime, my chief desire is to go on working as a psychic medium. I cannot think of a better way to spend my allotted time. All I want to do is spread the good news that, although our physical bodies may cease to function and our footprints disappear from the sand, our laughter no longer ripple and our tears leave no stain, there is nothing to fear in death. Something beautiful remains. We are *not* 'lost' and we do *not* 'lose' our loved ones. Life is eternal, and any one moment of life or death is but one moment that, in truth, stands still forever.

Tony Stockwell
Essex, 2004

I
Beginnings

I was standing in the middle of a battlefield. Wherever I looked there were bodies lying around, and the sound of the machine-gun fire, blood-curdling screams and groans was deafening. Some of the casualties were lying face-down on the tarmac; others, their eyes wide open, were gazing unseeingly at the sky; still more were crawling about on their knees or bellies. Bullets were ricocheting around the enclosed area, with its prefabricated buildings, and those who had just 'bought it' in the latest volley of gun fire were sinking slowly to the ground before rolling over and becoming yet another casualty of the war.

'NO!'

The voice that rang out above the noise was that of a seven-year-old child. Dressed in a black anorak and long charcoal-grey trousers, I had just experienced a vision in the school playground that I *had* to pass on.

'No – you *can't* be dead,' I cried out to my young classmates. 'You *can't* be dead.'

I knew the rules of this game, knew that when somebody aimed their fingers at you and muttered 'ak-ak-ak' or 'rata-tat-tat' and yelled 'You're dead', you had to go into instant death-throe mode, clutch at your throat or your chest, sink slowly to the ground and remain lying down until the school bell rang. I knew I was spoiling the fun, that my classmates would all think – and doubtless say – 'You're mad, Tony', but I didn't care. I had been stopped in my tracks, frozen to the spot by the images in my mind, and more than anything else in the world I

5

wanted these kids pretending to be dead to listen to me, to open their eyes, get up and understand that they *couldn't* die, that they could *never* die. I wanted them to know that what I had just seen in the vision was that we were all, each and everyone of us, eternal.

'You *can't* be dead,' I repeated over and over again, running frantically from one body to the next, shaking them by the shoulders. 'You can't be dead because we can't die – not now, not ever.'

'Shurrup', 'Sod off', 'Clear off', was the response to my first attempt to pass on a message from the spirit world!

Twenty-seven years later, I found myself in the middle of yet another battlefield. Surrounded by a camera crew, I was standing on a wild, rugged moor near Inverness in North Scotland. Here, in 1746, English militia under the command of Prince William, the obese Duke of Cumberland, had cut Bonnie Prince Charlie's Jacobites to shreds in what became known as the Battle of Culloden, one of the bloodiest battles ever fought. The night after the massacre, grieving wives and mothers, their shawls pulled tightly around their stooped shoulders, had stood wailing by the corpses of their loved ones.

In 2003, having been a medium for nearly fifteen years, I was on the moor filming for a television series entitled *Psychic School*. During a break in the shooting, which was taking place at midnight, I was suddenly overcome by an intense feeling that something, somebody, was tugging at my sleeve, determined to pull me further afield. Standing there, armed only with a small torch and aware that a heavy mist was settling in, the last thing I wanted to do was break away from the comforting presence of the group and move a hundred metres or so on to the pitch black, cold, misty moor, but I knew that scared though I was, there was something for me to do there; it was imperative that I should open up my psychic vision and become receptive.

For a few moments, although I felt a great chill encircling me, all seemed normal. Seconds later, all this changed. Suddenly, without warning, I was hurtled back to 1746, where foot soldiers, spurred on by the solemn beat of kettledrums, their regimental banners waving in the wind, were marching into battle. The sound of metal against metal as highlanders carrying broadswords and heavy studded shields struck terror into the English troops, was deafening, and the sound of cannon fire, drums beating, pipes playing and trumpets sounding was fearsome. With every new round of cannonade, thick black smoke billowed up in the air.

For what seemed like an eternity I was rooted to the spot, while all around me injured and dying men, Scotland's finest and bravest, some still clutching their shields and swords or muskets and powder horns, were being trampled deeper and deeper into the blood-soaked heather by those who were still advancing. Then, as I stood there, I sensed a presence just to the left of me and, looking into my mind's eye, I came face to face with a scruffy youth aged about sixteen. He had long, straggly ginger hair, was wearing a mud-splattered kilt, was shivering from the cold and was obviously petrified.

'Hallo,' he said, breathlessly. 'My name is Andrew.'

Shocked by the suddenness of his appearance, I somehow managed to answer, 'What have you come for? What do you want me to see?'

'Let me show you how I died,' he replied.

'I don't want to do this,' I thought, panicked, but the next moment I felt Andrew enter my body and I knew that I had to do as he bid and experience his last moments.

In truth I knew I was still rooted to the same spot, but I also knew that with nowhere to hide, with no safe refuge for man or beast on that savage moor, I was running – running as fast as my legs could carry me across the rain-sodden heather.

'Where's my father? Where's my father?' Andrew kept crying out, and I understood then that in the midst of that terrible battle this terrified youth had become separated from his father and, after his own death, had become emotionally, spiritually trapped in that place.

Moments later, now terror stricken myself, I became aware that there was a warrior directly behind me. Andrew was done for and I knew it. Weighed down by the heaviness of his wet clothes and drenched in his fear and sweat, I felt the man's breath on the nape of my neck, then as a hand grasped me by the shoulder and wrenched me to a halt, a lethally sharp blade slit my throat. The next moment Andrew had collapsed on to the earth, was lying face-down on the heather, choking on his own blood.

'*Please*,' I cried out to my spirit guides and to the Great Spirit, 'please release this boy from this place.'

My hands must have been outstretched and open because I felt someone lightly touch my palms.

'Andrew, go forward,' I cried, knowing it was my role as he lay dying to lift him up, release him, and help to send his spirit up into the light. 'Go into the light and be whole now.'

The next moment I felt that he had gone, had been rescued, and then there was nothing but a feeling of total exhaustion, of being utterly drained.

Seconds later, my eyes still closed, I became aware of total silence all around me. I was Tony Stockwell again. Opening my eyes, I peered into the mist, thinking, 'Oh God, where am I? What am I doing?' Then, as I came round, I realised it had been such a real experience that I was actually lying flat on my stomach on the heather, soaked to the skin.

My dying for Andrew wasn't a painful sensation, but it

contained the memory of pain, rather like when you cut your finger. After a few days the actual physical pain has gone, but you can clearly remember how the pain felt.

I had just performed what is known in the psychic world as a spirit rescue, and having waited a moment or two longer, I got up, brushed myself down and walked slowly back to where I had left the camera crew.

'Tony!' a member of the crew exclaimed, relieved to see me appear out of the mist. 'Where did you go? What happened? We couldn't see you anywhere.'

'Give me a moment,' I replied, 'then I'll record what I have just experienced on camera.'

Most people, I know, would consider the two events I have just described as strange, horrendous experiences. Many, I know, would mutter, 'We've got a right one here.' Others of a more charitable ilk might wonder if being at the receiving end of such heart-rending paranormal experiences would turn any normal person into somebody who needed psychiatric help. But I can only testify that I have never been left unbalanced by the paranormal events that have touched my life.

Even as a child, I somehow always knew I was different. Yet I was not the proverbial seventh son of a seventh son, the person who is said to be most likely to have unique gifts as a medium and be able to act as an intermediary between those who have gone on to the spirit world and those who are still in this world. My beginnings could not have been more ordinary.

Born in Walthamstow, East London, on 20 February 1969, the year now remembered for Concorde making its supersonic maiden flight and Neil Armstrong becoming the first man to walk on the moon, I couldn't have wished for better or more loving parents. My mum, Pat, who was born in the East End of London, met my dad, Keith, who was also born in East

London, at a local youth club when she was thirteen and he was fifteen. For them it really was young love, and Mum, completely smitten by my dad's good looks, lied about her age so that she and Dad could start going out together. Engaged at sixteen and married at eighteen, she had my sister, Lorraine, in 1966, and I came along when Mum was twenty-three.

Physically, I'm a patchwork of both of them. Dad, like me, is pale skinned and blond – although his beard is greyish now. A painter and decorator, he's a very fit East End barrow-boy, a salt-of-the-earth type of feller who has no airs and graces. Very street-wise, he fancies himself as a bit of a comedian. His humour can be rather sarcastic and even cutting at times, but he never means to be unkind.

A very glamorous fifty-something, my mum used to be a hairdresser but now works in a motel on Canvey Island, Essex, where I spent most of my childhood and early youth.

Theirs has always been a very happy marriage, and Dad, rather embarrassingly, has this habit of looking at my mum and saying, 'Your mum is *so* beautiful. Just look at your mum, Tony. Isn't she beautiful?'

Embarrassment to one side, I can only agree! She's lovely.

It's been great for me having such firm foundations. They've been really good, fun-loving parents, and the happiness they found in their marriage has certainly taught me a great deal about how to appreciate and get on with other people.

I spent my young childhood in Walthamstow, then when I was four, we moved to Canvey Island, thirty miles east of London, on the Essex coast, where my maternal great granddad had once owned a big boat and some land on 'the point' by the sea.

When we first moved to the island, we lived in a semi-detached house in Urmond Road where we stayed until I was fourteen.

It was while we were living there that I had one of my first paranormal experiences. In the early hours of the morning, when the house was in total darkness, I awoke to the sound of a woman's voice calling my name.

'T-o-n-y . . . T-o-n-y . . .'

As I lay there listening, I could not work out where this strange voice was coming from. Sometimes it seemed to be in the hallway just outside my bedroom; at other times it was very close, right by my left ear. Then, as the voice started to move around the room and out into the hall, fear got the better of me. Springing out of bed, I made a dash for safety across the hall into my parents' room.

Having climbed into bed with Mum and Dad, who were fast asleep, I lay there sandwiched between them. Slowly, as I began to feel more secure, I found the courage to raise my head and peer out into the hall through the crack in the open bedroom door. The voice was no longer calling me, but I was in for another shock. Staring straight at me through the banisters was the face of a young, dark-skinned woman, with the hood of a black cape pulled over her head. Absolutely petrified, I sank back under the sheets.

'Please God,' I murmured, 'make her go away.' I *really* wanted this woman, who I somehow knew was not of this world, to leave the house.

To this day, I have no idea who she was or why she was calling my name, and I never saw her again. She might just have been a spirit who was wandering around the neighbourhood. She might have heard other spirits talking about a boy who was receptive to spirits, but who was still very young. Perhaps she was just in a playful mood and felt like being mischievous. I shall never know.

We moved house several times after this and eventually ended up in Thorney Bay Road, where, joy of joy, we lived right opposite the sea.

The sea has always been very important to me, and even when we lived in flats or houses that didn't have a view of it, I'd always find my way to the seashore – or to the lake that is in the middle of the island. Water, whether it's in a garden pond, stream or lake, has a tremendous draw for me, but the sea is my passion.

I always thought Canvey Island was a very special place to live and grow up in, and I was always conscious that it was a place with a history. Even as a child, when I was wandering about the island on my own, I often caught fleeting images of people from a past age walking ahead or alongside me. I never questioned what I was seeing, or ever thought that this was strange in any way. I just accepted that it was happening and they were there. The ordinary houses and the streets would disappear before my eyes and, in their place, marshland occupied by people I now know to be Anglo-Saxons would appear. Sometimes, too, as I looked out to sea, I would catch the outlines of huge old sailing ships drifting past just offshore.

Looking back, I have no way of knowing whether these childhood experiences were created by my vivid imagination, or whether they were the first rich pickings of a person destined to be a psychic/medium.

We were a working-class family who never had any money to spare, yet I never felt deprived. My mum didn't tell me until quite recently that times were so hard for her and Dad that she often went without dinners in order to feed Lorraine and me. As we got older, though, my father got better jobs and my mother continued to work, so things did get easier, but we never had any money left over for luxuries. When we went on holiday, we nearly always went to my nan Kathleen's caravan at Maldon, Essex, which was not very far from home, but I really enjoyed going there.

When I was six years old, my dad gave me a fright that

could have scarred me for life. Having just sold his car, he drove it to the forecourt of the secondhand car dealer and parked it. Unbelievable though this may sound, in the midst of all the excitement he forgot that I was in the car, spreadeagled on the back seat, and got out and trotted off home without me. It wasn't until Mum returned from work and said, 'Where's Tony?' that he remembered me.

Mortified, he ran hell-for-leather back to the car, where I, having been abandoned for over two hours, was sitting bored out of my mind, my nose pressed up against the window pane, crying my eyes out. I guess it says something about me that, despite my anxiety attack after an hour or so of waiting for Dad to return, I had not even attempted to get out of the car. I can only imagine how the new owners would have felt had they come to collect the car and spotted the 'extra' that came along with it!

My dad was never allowed to forget his oversight. 'What kind of man is it', my mum used to joke, 'who tries to sell his only son along with his car?'

My first experience of illness and death was when I was seven. My granddad, Mum's dad, Bert, was a lovely gentleman, a very proud man who had been in the RAF. Always immaculately turned out, his shoes so polished you could see your face in them, he had a tiny Clark Gable moustache. In his younger days he had been a champion ballroom dancer, and whenever we visited him as a family, he would be sitting in his old brown leather armchair listening to Latin American music. Sometimes he had large headphones on, which Nan made him wear because she didn't like the music, and he'd be tapping his fingers and drumming his feet to the rhythm. When he left the RAF he made his living making sidecars for motorbikes and, given what happened to him, asbestos must have been used in their manufacture.

Ever since I could remember, Granddad had been breathless, but as a kid you don't take much notice of such things. One day, however, I was out in the car with him on a beautiful, sunny July afternoon, when I noticed that he was having great difficulty breathing.

'Granddad,' I said, displaying a wisdom greater than my years, 'you're not breathing properly. You should go to the doctor.'

'I've been to the doctor,' he replied, gently.

'And has he given you any medicine?' I asked.

He didn't reply, and to my surprise, when I next looked at him, I could see tears rolling down his cheeks. I was really upset, couldn't think what I had said or done to upset him, but once he had recovered, he managed to put everything right by saying, 'D'you fancy fish 'n chips and an ice-cream?'

I know now, of course, that he knew he was dying of asbestosis, the terrible lung disease that's caused by breathing in asbestos dust, but he just couldn't tell a seven-year-old boy.

Just before he died three months later, in October of that year, a time when everybody was talking about Christmas presents and the festivities, he asked to see me. When I arrived at his home, which was my nan's pride and joy because she was always winning first prize for the magnificent display of flowers in her front garden, there he was lying in bed, an oxygen mask on his face. The curtains were drawn, but there was sufficient light for me to see that he was very weak, hardly able to lift a finger or speak, but he was determined, however long it took, to manage a few words.

'What . . . do . . . you . . . want . . . for Christmas?' he asked.

'Hm? What do I want?' I remember thinking, then, inspired, I said, 'I know, Granddad. I want a watch.'

Having heard this, he smiled and tried to raise his hand and remove his watch from his wrist. It was a beautiful, solid gold watch, presented to him as a retirement present by his employer. As he struggled to pull it off, my mum and my nan, seeing how much discomfort this was causing him, begged him not to struggle any more.

I am left with such a strong vision of standing at the foot of the bed, watching my granddad, who was all skin and bone at this stage, struggling to take off his watch and give it to me for my Christmas present. He could hardly move, could hardly catch his breath, but he wanted to do it himself and tried so hard before having to give up. That was one of the saddest moments of my childhood.

Later, I learned that just before he died, he made Nan and Mum promise that when he was gone, I would have the watch, and that's what happened.

Over the years, several mediums have given me messages from him, and it has always been the mention of his gold watch and small Clark Gable moustache that has clinched his presence for me. Likewise, whenever I have been at my lowest ebb emotionally, and feel that I need special help from the spirit world, it is nearly always my granddad whose presence I feel at my side. He was sixty-five when he died, had only just retired, but whenever I see his presence clairvoyantly, I always feel he is much younger than his years and he always looks very healthy and happy.

They were good people, my granddad and nan, and I was very lucky to have my nan in my life until she died of cancer when I was seventeen.

I also had a very close relationship with my dad's parents. My dad's mum was called Bessy, but she always insisted on being called Betty. Although she came from the most awful background and was taken into care as a child, she really made something of herself. A very proper lady who spoke well, she had been seriously abused at a young age. Her mother used to stab her, and the scars from these attacks were still visible even when Betty was an adult. They'd faded over the years, but I am sure they were just as deep inside. I never met my dad's biological father, who left my nan and went to live in Spain many years before I was born, so my paternal grandfather was my dad's step-father, Ron, Betty's second husband. Ron, who is still alive, has always been a true granddad to me.

The other person who was very important to me, and who has now passed, was my nan's sister, my Aunt Grace, who lived close to us in a pretty, spic-and-span bungalow that always had gorgeous hanging baskets in its front garden. I was so lucky because we saw her all the time. Married to Roy, she was a very, witty, vibrant character who drank like a fish, smoked like a chimney and swore like a navvy, but she was always a lady and absolutely my favourite person. She used to say to me, 'What's your favourite swear word? Mine's bol-locks. I *love* that word.' Both my nan and Aunt Grace were very glamorous East End ladies who looked like Elsie Tanner from *Coronation Street* – all backcombing, hairspray, perfume and fags. They were such fun to be around.

Although I miss my grandparents and Aunt Grace terribly, I know I haven't lost them because I still see and hear them. Even now, as I write this book, I can feel their presence in the room. It's not that they want to say anything in particular to me at this moment, they are just enfolding me in the warmth of their love. I am so blessed to have a psychic gift and to be able to sense them. This may sound very strange, but as more and more people who have been close to me pass on, I feel stronger. This is because they do not disappear into a great abyss. They remain with me, are always there as an unseen support and back-up. It really is a blessing to know that the power of love can transcend even death. Death, for me, is simply a passing from one room to another, one existence to another. We and our loved ones are eternal.

It also seems entirely natural to me that the moment we discover we have survived death, we want to get this reassuring message back to those we have left behind. We want them to know that there is nothing to fear, that death has no sting, and grave no victory.

2

First Meetings

One of my earliest memories is what I now know to be an out-of-body, astral-projection experience. My mum had just put me down in my cot, one of those old-fashioned wooden jobs that had white bars and bunny rabbit motifs on it, and, although I was only three, I remember thinking I really was very clever because I could get out of my cot and my mum would never know. What I used to do as soon as she went out of the room was to let my body vibrate. I don't think I physically vibrated, but my spirit certainly did, and I then willed myself out of the cot to float first around the tiny boxroom, then down the narrow stairs into my parents' lounge, where I would hover at ceiling height or just sit on the back of an armchair and watch them. It was comforting to watch Mum doing the ironing while Dad watched telly or read the paper.

For me, my spirit hovering outside my body and floating up and downstairs was perfectly natural, and I enjoyed rather than feared the experience. It was very exciting to know that when Mum put me down in the cot, I could be out again within seconds if I wasn't sleepy, and that when I became tired I could float back to my cot and gaze at my bunny rabbits while I settled down for the night.

Sadly, I lost this ability as I grew up and I don't remember ever doing it again after we left Walthamstow and moved to the island. Many years then passed before I realised that I was still capable of having out-of-body experiences and I have actually done this on three memorable occasions since I became an adult.

When I think back on my sun-sea-and-sand childhood, I realise how lucky I was to grow up in such a congenial place. If I had lived in a town or city, where people's senses are constantly bombarded and overloaded, I might have become rather unreceptive and missed out on developing the psychic side of my nature. Certainly, I have never felt truly in tune with myself when surrounded by nothing but miles and miles of concrete, noise and bustle.

Born under the star sign of Pisces, I'd like to think that, even as a child, I had a goodly number of the characteristics that astrologers list under that sign. Many of them do seem to fit my own experience of myself. Pisceans are thought to be very deep people who, while given to raging passions, are inclined to bottle things up, be secretive, and are therefore among the most misunderstood members of the zodiac. By nature, they are kind, loving, trusting and forgiving, and willing to work very hard for those they love – and even for those they don't like that much! Often backward in coming forward, they're inclined to lurk in the shadows until opportunities arise for them to come into their own. Then they can be friendly, chatty and charismatic. Because they are deep thinkers, who are blessed with natural intuition and a sensitivity which gives them the ability to weigh up the pros and cons of any situation, and because they have an innate desire to help those who are suffering or in trouble, other people tend to confide in them and often describe them as psychic!

I must say that when I come across these kinds of summaries in astrology books or newspaper columns, I often feel I am being presented with a scarily accurate self-portrait!

Certainly, I was the kind of kid who was sensitive to others, and I definitely wanted to help people. My mum is fond of telling one particular story which illustrates this. Always a bit of a loner, who didn't make friends very easily, I enjoyed playing out in the street with the few boys who were my mates – boys who were inclined to be quiet, like me. Sometimes when I was trotting about with them in a road not far from our house that had little bungalows on both sides, I noticed a very old lady – she must have been all of ninety – peeping out from behind her net curtains and watching us. Her skin really was all peaches and cream, and her silvery-white hair was back-combed and as wispy as the candyfloss that we bought along the promenade. She always had a beaming smile on her face and made a point of returning my waves.

One day, trotting down that road as usual, I suddenly got it into my head that she looked very tired and I wanted to help her. Abandoning my friends, I ran all the way back to my empty house. Once inside I removed a pound of butter, a pint of milk and some slices of ham from the fridge, then bearing these trophies I hurried as fast as my legs would carry me to the old lady's little pink bungalow.

Holding the gifts aloft so that she could see them, I lifted the latch of her garden gate and then stood waiting by the front door. She took forever to shuffle in her carpet slippers from her lounge, along the linoleum-clad passageway, to the front door, but when she opened it her face was wreathed in smiles. Making it clear that she was absolutely thrilled to see me standing there, she indicated that I should carry the goodies through to her lounge. I don't remember her saying anything other than, 'Thank you, darlin', I'll have a *lovely* tea tonight', but I have never forgotten her smile. I also remember that when I walked back down her garden path after placing the goods on the brown formica table in her lounge, I felt ten feet tall.

It was a different story, when Mum came home that night.

'Who?', 'What?', 'Where?' was the order of the evening, followed by a puzzled, 'Tony, have you been taking stuff from the fridge?'

I was tempted to lie, but I somehow knew that would make matters worse and I settled for telling the truth.

'You what?' she said a few times, clearly astonished, but then as the reality sank in, she sat quietly for a moment without saying anything. Then, she didn't tell me off, didn't give me a hiding, didn't give me any kind of punishment. She somehow managed to convey to me that although we could ill afford the loss of the butter, the milk and the ham, and that we would now go short ourselves, I had done a good thing – something really nice.

'That was a very kind thought,' she said, 'but don't ever take things from the fridge again, love, without asking first.'

That is so like my mum. A sensitive lady with a heart of gold, she has always had a sound sense of right and wrong.

Sometime later I found myself walking past the little pink bungalow again. When I saw the old lady in the window, she smiled and waved to me in the usual way and I smiled and waved back.

'That ham must really have done her good,' I thought. 'She doesn't look at all tired now. She looks *really* healthy.'

When I returned home, I told my mum that I had seen the old lady again, and that she had looked lovely and had waved to me.

Mum stopped what she was doing and looked at me.

'Are you sure it was the old lady's bungalow?' she asked.

'Yes,' I replied, puzzled. 'It was the pink one.'

'Well, I'm very surprised,' Mum replied gently. 'One of our neighbours told me last week that your lovely old lady had died.'

It was true. A month later, I saw new people moving their furniture into the old lady's bungalow.

My first meeting with a spirit who manifested as an image – a vision – outside rather than inside my head, was on a very hot summer's day. I was seven years old, one of a group of six boys who loved walking for miles and playing on the beach. At that time there were some old Second World War gun-placements on the sea wall that looked out over the estuary, and we loved mucking around near them and catching out courting couples!

One particularly large gun-placement had a door at each end, and we used to play a game called 'chicken', in which we had to prove our bravery by going in one door on our own and seeing how quickly we could run to the other end through the pitch-black interior without falling over or getting scared out of our wits. If we refused to do this, we were named and shamed, while all the others made clucking 'chicken' noises around us. I must have done the run a dozen times before, so I was pretty blasé about the whole business, but on this occasion, as I ran towards the middle of the gun-placement, I was in for a shock.

It was always black as midnight in there, but this time it seemed even darker, and there in the middle of this darkness was an orange glow that was getting bigger and bigger the closer I came to it. As I slowed down to a walk, then to a stop, the orange glow suddenly cleared and immediately in front of me, large as life, was a man sitting behind an old-fashioned, dark wooden desk, writing in an old leather-bound book. I knew that he was writing with a quill pen and, young as I was, I remember thinking as it made scratching sounds on the paper that this was odd, because if he was a ghost belonging to the Second World War when the gunney was built, he wouldn't be writing with a quill pen!

The image and the surroundings didn't quite match up, but I knew what I was seeing and, as I stood there, he suddenly became aware of me and looked up.

Although I sensed he was a friendly presence and knew I had nothing to fear, I was a bit apprehensive and decided to make a run for it to the end of the building and out into the brightness of the day.

Once outside, feeling somewhat stunned, I beckoned my friends over.

'You'll never guess what,' I said, and as soon as I had stopped panting, more from shock than from running, I tried to explain the vision that had appeared before my eyes.

They listened politely enough, but none of them was in the least bit interested or impressed, and they soon went back to skimming pebbles over the tops of the frothy waves or looking for knife- or gun-shaped pieces of driftwood on the seashore.

Later, I remember walking home with my closest mate, Mark, and saying, 'You know what, I think I saw a ghost.' But even as he nodded, I was more certain than that. I *knew* I had seen a ghost; was totally convinced I had seen a ghost.

Years later, when I was in my early twenties, I went for a psychic reading – a one-to-one sitting with a medium – and included in the information I was given that day was the fact that I had once seen a vision of a man writing in a book with a quill pen.

'That's absolutely correct,' I said.

'His name is Pierre,' the medium replied, 'and he wants you to know that he is a guide of yours and that one day he wishes to write through you.'

I thought this was a wonderful piece of synchronicity, and I was very impressed that, so many years later, a medium could give me this information without knowing anything about my childhood experience.

From that moment on, I started to do what in psychic circles is called 'automatic writing'. This is when a medium holds a pen, looks away, and the pen moves on its own; the words just come. Pierre has not yet become a major spirit guide of mine, but I have used automatic writing from time to time in my work and people have confirmed the accuracy of the information they have received.

In 2003 I was doing a one-to-one reading for a young woman. It was a perfectly straight-forward reading in which I just happened to be holding a pen and pad of paper. While we were talking, I felt the pen start to move in my hand and the name Wayne appeared on the paper.

'Who's Wayne?' I asked.

'A boy who died in our street,' she replied at once.

Looking down again, I saw that the pen had written the words 'on bike'.

'Was he on his bike?' I queried.

'Yes,' she replied, stunned. 'He was riding his bike when he was killed.'

The pen was now moving again and this time the name Barry appeared.

'Who's Barry?' I asked.

'Oh my God,' she cried out. 'He was my sister's boyfriend.'

When I next glanced at the paper three more words had come through: 'head-on crash'.

'Did he die in a head-on crash?' I asked.

By now, the young lady was crying.

'Yes,' she gulped through her tears.

The next two pieces of information on the paper were the number 19 and the name Lorraine.

'My sister is Lorraine,' the girl sobbed when I presented her with these, 'and she was nineteen when her boyfriend died in the crash.'

These words had appeared simply because I was holding pen and paper and the spirit who was present had chosen this way to communicate with us.

Automatic writing may not give a whole message, but the words that come through during readings are very significant to the person concerned. If a spirit wants – needs – to get a message through, he or she will do so in any way they can. This may be through a voice, in a vision, or in the writing of a word.

'Darlings,' they are saying, 'we are not dead, you haven't lost us, we are here.'

I know many people say that they would be scared if they saw a spirit, but I try to explain that it's not just the *seeing* of the spirit that counts, but the *feeling* that the spirit brings with them. For me, it's often a feeling of being totally enveloped in love, honoured and cared for, and there is no fear whatsoever. On some occasions I have experienced a different kind of energy – the 'chill' that people talk about – but on the whole my experiences have been positive. In truth, there is nothing to fear, not even from a negative spirit, because mind is the most powerful tool that we are given to use on this earth and we can use it to discriminate between negative and positive experiences. As the poet John Milton said in 'Paradise Lost':

> *The mind is its own place and in itself*
> *Can make a Heav'n of hell, a Hell of Heav'n.*

If we do sense a negative presence, all we have to do is say, 'I don't want this particular spirit around me.' Then, turning to the spirit, we can say, 'OK, thank you for coming, but now go on your way.' If you starve them of attention, they will not stay!

* * *

One day when I was twelve, my mum and my Auntie Sue were sitting around our kitchen table using a ouija board which they had made by writing letters of the alphabet on squares of paper and placing these into a circle on the table. They put an upturned glass into the centre of the letters and placed their fingers on top of it as they had seen my nan do many years before. It was only meant to be a bit of fun and they were both very giggly because, by that point in the evening, they had had a fair amount to drink. You can only imagine their astonishment when the glass started to move of its own accord and a woman, who was obviously in the spirit world, came through and spelled out E-M-I-L-Y.

By this time, I had become interested and had just gone to sit alongside them when my dad and Uncle Ian – Auntie Sue's husband – came back from the pub.

'What the bleedin' hell . . . ?' Dad said as he walked in through the kitchen door.

As he said this, the glass, which moments before had been picking up speed and shooting around the letters of the alphabet, shot off the table and smashed on the floor at his feet.

Dad, who was rather shaken by this, promptly sat down and didn't say another word!

Mum and Auntie Sue had no knowledge of any Emily in the family and they went on giggling and being silly. But when they told my nan about the experience, they were in for a shock.

'Emily,' Nan told them, 'was my mum, your nan, who died before you were born.'

It was their turn to be shaken, but I thought it was wonderful that Emily had cared enough to communicate with us via the ouija board.

Dad remained chastened: 'I'll never swear in front of her again!'

There has only ever been one occasion when I resisted my 'calling' to all things spiritual, and this was when I was fourteen. I remember kicking my heels against the bed in my room and thinking: 'I *don't* believe in God. I *don't* believe in anything. I reckon when we die, we die'.

I kind of enjoyed that feeling of rebellion for about a day, but the spirits must have been with me even then because, in my heart of hearts, I knew it was not true.

There were lots of times before – and after – that experience when I just wanted to be close to religion in a Catholic or Anglican church or a synagogue – it did not matter which. I had this overwhelming need to serve and I just wanted to get on my knees, be devout, pay homage and be very humble in the presence of this all-powerful being.

Many years later, I received a message from a vibrant, fun-loving, Jewish medium called Betty de Rose. 'If you had not gone in to mediumship,' she said, 'you would have become a monk or a priest.'

As soon as she said that, I thought: 'Yes – she's absolutely right. I've always had this need to do something on the path of service, and I always wanted to do this within a religious context.'

It's true. Even though I might sometimes appear to be the most unreligious kind of person, who still behaves like a bit of a yob and swears far too often, there has always been a part of me that has craved a monastic way of life – walking through cloisters fragranced by incense, summoned by bells and chanting endless prayers. I am also drawn to the Buddhist way of worship because I love the ritual – the beads, the prayers, the meditation and the mantras.

Around the same time as my short-lived rebellion, I also remember five of us – my friend Jason, my sister and her two friends – being in Jason's house swapping ghost stories. I wasn't into sex or establishing the facts of life at that point, but I was certainly into ghost stories, and I was so excited that afternoon, my head was all fuzzy.

All of a sudden, in the middle of a story, Jason's record player switched itself on and started to belt out music at top volume.

We did not like that one little bit and each of us was petrified and shrieked aloud – but it was kind of nice to be so scared!

In general, my mum and dad were so busy earning our daily crust that I don't think they were really aware that I was different from other boys. They both worked incredibly hard and, like most parents, were just regular people who were learning how to be parents as they went along.

I was always a passionate child, but I don't think I ever had a strong urge to tell my mum what I was experiencing and feeling, and maybe that's because I wasn't that articulate when I was young. I just kept things to myself and went with the flow. Occasionally I would slide up to her when she was getting our tea ready or flicking a duster over a sideboard to tell her that I had seen a spirit or heard voices, but she never made a big deal of this and never made me feel I was strange. She would just look at me in that matter-of-fact way that parents reserve for their kids and say, 'Oh, well, maybe it was a ghost you saw, then?' Looking back, I know she was just humouring me, but at the time it meant everything.

I can also remember several occasions from early childhood onwards when I would turn to Mum and share a recurring feeling or thought.

'I don't know why, Mum,' I'd say, 'but I feel as if I've been born to do something different.'

'Maybe you have,' she'd reply as she tucked me into bed, brushed my hair or gave me a kiss. 'Maybe you will become a doctor or inventor or something like that and do great things.'

I realise now that my mum is what we psychics call 'a sensitive'; that is, she was blessed with a sixth sense, an all-encompassing knowingness that comes over us mediums rather like a vast umbrella that enables us to hear and speak to dead people. The sixth sense is a power that is way beyond those of our normal senses and it allows us to perceive things that we couldn't possibly manage with our other five senses.

Often when I am with my mum, I sense that she could have been a medium if she had developed her sensitivity to a point where she was able to work with it, but her life never took that course. Now Lorraine and I are grown up, though, she has more time to look into psychic matters. She – and Dad – are my most loyal supporters and give me so much encouragement.

I had many happy times in my childhood, but one memory that stands out was when I was twelve and on a family holiday in Cornwall with my mum, dad and sister, and we were joined by Auntie Sue and Uncle Ian, and their two sons Scott and Kevin – my favourite cousins.

I can't remember which part of Cornwall we were in, but it was a very rugged area and we four kids were exploring a sandy beach and pebble-dashed shoreline while our mums were sunbathing and our dads were propping up a bar somewhere. The beach was fringed by caves and there were lots of fascinating rockpools full of fronds of seaweed that looked like the fingers of a green hand, and barnacles, clams and sea anemones, and while I was busy gazing into one of these, I must have got left behind by the others. When I next became conscious of where I was, I had left the beach and waded knee-deep through water into a cave.

As I reached the back of this dank, dark cavern and turned round to look back through the gloom to the brilliant sunshine just beyond its mouth, I became aware that it was no longer me who was looking through my eyes. There was another being present, who was using my eyes to take in the brightness of the sparkling scene beyond. I felt much older, was suddenly about six feet tall with a beard. I wasn't frightened; I was elated, happy that I was able to let this being look through my eyes.

At the time, I was just totally accepting – receptive – without really comprehending what was happening. I didn't realise until much later in life, when I was a member of a psychic development group, that heavenly bodies, like the one who had come to me, sometimes use humans as a vessel to allow them to return and gaze upon the earth and all its beauty.

Thanks to that visitation, though, the sense that I had in the cave that day was one of total bliss, of being connected with nature, completely unified with the elements, earth, air, fire, water and ether.

About four years ago I had a similar experience in Gran Canaria, when I was swimming in the sea, but this time there was not another spirit present. Suddenly lifted into a state of total unity with my surroundings, I felt the current of water moving around my body, the sandy bed of the Atlantic Ocean beneath my feet connecting me to the earth, the heat of the sun on my shoulders, the wind blowing across my face, the huge skies above. All the elements were in place and I felt completely and utterly in tune with nature. This experience only lasted for thirty seconds, but while it did I felt I could see and hear for a million miles beyond my normal vision and hearing and I was totally and utterly in sync with the universe.

The thought then came to me that there was no reason why we couldn't be in that state of perfection, of all-encompassing knowing, more often. All that is needed is the ability to be receptive, to open up our five senses and completely surrender to whatever the moment brings. With openness, surrender and acceptance in situ, we could experience more frequent moments of total harmony with the universe and nature. The reason we do not is that for most of the time we are a closed shop, fragmented like a kaleidoscope, in a state of flux, experiencing annoyance, self-pity or anger, living in the past or living in the future, but never quite living, moment by moment, in the present.

Basically, we forget we have a divine as well as a human nature. We limit ourselves to this or that feeling or worry, this or that life move, and get weighted down by flesh-and-bones matters. Yet when we lose sight of the reality of who and what we are, and forget that we have a beautiful spirit inside, we impede our own progress, our ability to grow through this life's experiences. For instance, even if we are in a very difficult situation, we can accept the fact that it is difficult and learn to work through it, or we can leave it behind us and move on. It is this acceptance, this willingness to learn from what confronts us, that can result in a painful negative experience only lasting for a matter of weeks or months before a change for the better comes into being.

It's certainly been my experience in life that nothing is more important than the people and the teachers that we share our days with from childhood onwards.

As far as my education was concerned, I was reasonably well taught from five to eleven when I attended schools on Canvey Island. When I was in the third year of the juniors I had the most wonderful teacher, who had a great effect on my life, and I have never forgotten her. Her name was Mrs Payne. A very well spoken, forthright lady who never talked down to us and who brought us the most delicious juicy cherries from a tree in her garden, she regularly took us out of our stuffy classroom to visit a nearby pond. Once there, she would gather us in a quiet circle and point things out and talk to us about tadpoles, frogs, newts, dragonflies, water beetles and other forms of wildlife. In the spring she would take us off to a field that ran along the front of our school and show us the first crocuses coming up from the ground. She was a deeply sensitive woman in her early forties who would tell us tales about her own Essex childhood and about the things she had seen and done in her life. She had a great impact on me because she talked about the wonder of simple things, and I have always been indebted to her for that. She taught us about nature, life and humanity.

There was an ancient, dilapidated church on the island which was no longer used, and Mrs Payne and a group of her colleagues managed to get permission to run it as a heritage centre. My great joy, then, was to meet her at this church on Saturdays to be given jobs like sweeping out the building. I never minded the clouds of dust that got up my nostrils and clogged my throat because entering that place was like walking back in time and being in the presence of the benign spirits who had once worshipped there. I remember Mrs Payne taking the time to tell me about the various sections of the church – the pulpit, the altar, the nave – and she outlined the stories that were depicted on the stained glass windows, some of which were broken, some intact. Every time I visited that church, I had a real sense of having come home, of being in the presence of kindred spirits, of not wanting to leave.

Unlike my infant and junior schools, I did not like my senior school from the day I first set foot in there. I was a quiet boy surrounded by boisterous kids and I found the atmosphere much too bullish and aggressive. There was a lot of bullying in the school when I was there and some kids lives were made a living hell. I got off lightly, but I was always very conscious of the need to keep my head down and not antagonise anyone.

I am sure some of the other kids were aware that I was different, but, in general, I was accepted as an 'OK kid'. Fortunately I had some good mates who I had a lot in common with, and I was also on friendly terms with some really tough boys, who I had known since junior school. This certainly worked in my favour and earned me some respect.

Whatever the reason, I wasn't picked on or bullied any more than anyone else, but there was always the fear that I would be singled out and that I wouldn't be able to cope with it. In reality, though, I only had one really nasty experience, and that was when I was in the third year. One day, for no particular reason that I can recall, real hard case, one of the hardest boys in the school, came looking for me.

'I'm gonna have a fight with you after school,' he grunted, bunching his fists.

I was petrified. It was one of the worst days of my life, and having been given an advance warning, I had the entire day to fret about it. By the time the school day was over, there was no blood left in my veins and the whole school knew that this tough guy was going to kick the crap out of me.

'What are you gonna do?' my mates kept asking me. 'Are you gonna run, go to the Head, what?'

I don't know where the power came from, but suddenly I knew what I was going to do.

'I'm just gonna fight him,' I said.

'Fight him?' they echoed, their mouths agape. 'You're mad! He'll slaughter you.'

'Maybe. But I'm gonna fight him.'

So, white as a sheet and leaden-legged, but aware of a power, an energy, a force that was not my own coursing through my body, I walked into the playground at the dreaded hour. There, larger than life, ringed by onlookers, stood my tousle-haired tormentor, his fists clenched, ready to carry out his threat.

'Run, Tony – *run*,' a boy urged.

But determined to see it through, I stood in the centre of the circle, looked the bully straight in the eye and squared up to him.

To my – and everybody else's – astonishment, he returned my gaze for a moment, then, pulling a face that was meant to terrify all and sundry, he turned on his heel and sauntered off.

'What happened?' everybody was thinking, perplexed.

'What's the trick?' one boy asked.

'What did you do to him?' another enquired. 'How did you do that?'

I didn't know, didn't have any answers I could put into words. My heart was still thumping away and I wasn't aware of having done anything in particular. I'd just known that if I went to the Head, it would only delay the inevitable; and that if I'd run away, he would have kept on coming back until he caught me. The only way to deal with bullies, an inner voice had told me, was to face up to them.

There's no doubt about it, secondary schools can be very frightening places for a lot of sensitive people, and the experience of being persecuted and shattered by people's cruel jibes and vicious actions is responsible for a lot of pain and unfinished business when we are adults.

Later in life I came across an ancient Hindu story that threw light on what I had been through in the playground. A prince, the story goes, lived with his people in abject misery and poverty in a valley because the only entrance in or out was guarded by a huge dragon who breathed fire upon anyone who tried to pass. One day, when all the valley's resources were finally used up, the prince decided he had no choice but to lead his people out of the valley to the lush, verdant meadows beyond or they would all be doomed, would starve to death. Having marshalled his subjects into a long line behind him, he marched them toward the entrance of the valley, but, true to form, the dragon reared up and breathed his fiery breath upon them. Terrified, the prince and his people fell back, but once the prince had recovered he tried again, and then again, with the same results. On the last occasion, however, he noticed something different about the dragon. He noticed that every time he and his people took a step backwards, the dragon *increased* in size, but every time he and his people stepped forwards, the dragon got *smaller*. Suddenly, with renewed zeal, the prince stepped forwards and this time, ignoring the fiery blasts that singed his hair, he continued to go forwards. With each step, the dragon became smaller and smaller until eventually there was only something the size of a pea lying on the ground. Stooping down, the prince swooped the tiny creature into his hand.

'Who are you?' he asked, bewildered.

'Fear,' the creature replied.

Then the prince understood that it is fear that keeps us in bondage – in poverty of spirit – and that it is only the willingness to face up to our fears that will set us free.

With no more ado, he led his people out of poverty into the richness of the valley beyond.

The only time I was happy at senior school was when I was in the fifth year and I was offered the lead as Nicholas Necrophiliac in the play *Dracula Spectacular*. I loved that because I seemed to spend all year painting scenery and attending rehearsals with other kids in the drama group. The young girl who played Nadia Naive in the play was a friend of mine, Kim Guzzan, and some time after she left school she became a medium herself. We kept in touch for several years, even after she went to live in Scotland, but about four years ago she was killed in a road accident in Inverness.

When, Jan, her mother, eventually tracked me down with the tragic news, she said, 'I was in such a terrible state after Kim died that I decided to ring one of the psychic telephone lines. I eventually got through to a medium called Molly Bryant who said, without me having told her a single detail, "I've got your daughter here with me. She died very recently and her name is Kim. She wants to send her love to you and her dad, and to her brother and sister."'

'It really was the most perfect reading,' Jan then confided in me, 'because Molly Bryant told me so many accurate things that she could not have known if Kim had not come through to her.'

I was not at all surprised. Kim was a very believing girl, who was not only physically beautiful, she had a beautiful spirit, too, and I know she would have wanted to ease her mother's pain and let her and the rest of her family know that she was OK. This, for me, was a perfect example of a spirit wanting to convey something and then seizing an opportunity to communicate from beyond the grave.

Thanks to drama, then, I managed my final year at senior school, but I still couldn't wait to get out of there. I succeeded in getting a handful of O-levels, then, with a huge sigh of relief, I left school when I was sixteen.

For most youngsters of that age, getting your first job, starting work and being able to finger notes and jingle coins from your first pay packet is excitement enough. But something was about to happen to me that put all that into perspective – into second place.

3
On Probation!

When I was sixteen and just about to leave school, my sister's friend Mandy told me something that made my hair stand on end. Mandy had been to see a medium in a local Spiritualist church and the medium had spoken to 'dead people'.

I could hardly contain my excitement. 'Take me there,' was my instant reaction. I couldn't wait, I wanted to go right at that very moment.

By then I had seen Margaret Rutherford playing a medium in the classic film *Blithe Spirit*, and although that was the limit of my knowledge of mediumship at that time, seeing her conducting a séance and speaking to spirit people resonated very strongly with something within me.

'It's true, then,' I thought, when I overheard Mandy speaking to Lorraine, 'I'm not the *only* person who's aware of spirits and can hear their voices in my head. Other people hear voices and talk to the dead.'

At that time my nan, Kath, was very ill with lung cancer, and Mandy, who was a sensitive girl, had realised that I was even more interested than usual in life-and-death matters and invited me to go along with her to the next meeting.

I could hardly believe my ears. Older sister's friends are not in the habit of inviting young brothers to join them. On the contrary, they usually do everything to avoid them!

All that week, I remember feeling *very* excited, and I was so relieved when Sunday evening finally arrived. The Spiritualist meetings were held in an old Red Cross hall. Constructed of wood and plaster, it smelled of damp pine and was spartanly furnished with brown rickety chairs. When we arrived, there were already about thirty people present and the atmosphere, despite the smell, was friendly and warm.

The medium, a very ordinary looking lady dressed in a brown sweater and pleated skirt, gave an opening address, then invited us all to sing a hymn.

'This is great,' I thought, and by the time the medium began her talk about light, love and spirituality, I was feeling quite relaxed. The next moment, though, when she said she would give a demonstration, my heart started bruising my ribs and I felt sick with nervous anticipation.

Crossing the hall, she stood for a moment, her head on one side, as if listening to a far-off voice, then, opening her eyes, she alighted on a middle-aged lady whose dyed blonde hair was peeping out of a paisley headscarf.

'I'd like to come to this lady here,' she said in a loud, clear voice. 'I believe your husband is in the spirit world. He sends his love, asks if you had a lovely Christmas, and did you remember Billy and Johnny?'

The woman in the headscarf gasped, then said 'yes', 'no', 'I don't remember' or 'absolutely correct' to other bits of the message.

The meeting continued in this vein for forty minutes or so, with the medium moving from this person to that, and although I shrank in my seat, afraid that she would pick on me, I was completely spellbound.

'This woman is speaking to *dead* people,' I kept reminding myself, but far from feeling spooked, I felt as if the first sixteen years of my life had meant something, had been leading me to this moment, this place, and that I had now come home and knew what I was meant to do with my life.

Years before, when I had said to my mum that I felt as if I'd been born to do something different, she had suggested I might become a doctor or an inventor, but I now knew I was not intended to be either of these things. If, as I sensed, I *did* have a gift and I *was* blessed with the ability to be aware of spirits and hear their voices, this was the path I was intended to travel.

That night – and for many days and nights to come – I could think of nothing other than what I had witnessed and heard in the Red Cross hall. While my mates were celebrating leaving school and escaping from the four walls of our classroom, I couldn't wait to get back to the four walls of that little hall the following Sunday evening.

For two years after that first meeting, I went on my own every week, trudging the three miles to the hall in rain, wind, snow and ice. I was totally devoted to those evenings and I loved the prayers and the hymns.

During those two years, though, there was always a point in the meeting when I would sit there petrified, praying that the medium would not pick on me and give me a message. Then, as I became more confident and got to know some of the other people who attended, I became much less afraid of being placed in the spotlight, and one Sunday I actually said to myself, 'I'm ready now – I'd like a message.'

Unbelievably, that was the evening I was singled out to receive one, and after that I got one the next week and the week after that. It was always the same message: 'You have been guided here; you are a medium. We are going to work with you.'

I was astonished, but curiously calm and elated. I knew for sure then that mediumship was my vocation. By then I knew that a medium was a person who could be used as a vessel through which dead people – spirits – could communicate on a mind-to-mind level to bring messages of comfort to their loved ones. I also knew from my attendances at the meetings that, provided the medium was open and receptive, spirits could blend their minds with the medium's and there was no limit to the passing on of thoughts, emotions and inspiration; that if things were going really well, boundless information could be received. Above all, though, I knew I had much to learn before I could even begin to fulfil my vocation.

In our work, you do not leave school and become a medium. We have to make our way in the world, get a job like everybody else, and when I was seventeen, I did just that. I began work as a trainee sales executive for Brown and Tawes, which manufactured pipes and tubes for the building trade and was based in Bromley by Bow in the east end of London.

I hated my first job and longed for the freedom to get on with everything to do with mediumship, but the job was a means to an end. Work also gave me a structure and taught me discipline and how to get on with people from different walks of life, and I am far more feet-on-the-ground, focused and disciplined because of that work experience.

While I was at Brown and Tawes, I used to sit facing a grey filing cabinet that was placed just in front of my desk. For several months when I looked up from my work, I noticed little lights appearing on the cabinet. At first I thought I was seeing things, then I thought my eyes weren't focusing properly, but one day I came across a passage in a book headed 'Spirit Lights'. Suddenly what I was seeing in that office clicked into place. The lights which kept dancing around the filing cabinet were spirit lights.

These were early days in the development of my mediumship and I was thrilled that spirits were appearing to me in this light form. Spirit lights are little living lights that appear in lots of different shapes and forms. They may flicker for just a split second then disappear, or may remain for a long time, or even take up permanent residence in a room. They are not to be confused with sunspots which appear when, having gazed at the sun for too long, our eyes go fuzzy and spots appear. Spirit lights are of an entirely different order. They're vivid sparks of light that sometimes turn a vibrant shade of blue, like the spark of an electric current. They also appear as pristine white and very occasionally as orange glow lights.

Now that I have learned how to tune into their energy, I always know when somebody or something is present in a room, and when I tune more deeply into the light, I see the form of the spirit person within that light.

Sometimes spirits present themselves in this light form because they want to make it easier for us humans to know they are around; although they want to be seen, they have no particular wish to communicate with us in words. It is as if they are just content to enter a space and be perceived as light.

I am sure a lot of people see these lights, but they don't always realise what they are. Since those early occasions at Brown and Tawes, I have seen them a lot – day and night. There is one present in the room with me at this moment.

My first out-of-body experience as an adult, one that involved a glimpse of a previous life, took place when I was about seventeen years old.

Before I relate this experience, I would like to reassure people that reincarnation does *not* mean that we lose our loved ones. Reincarnation – when a spirit chooses to be reborn and returns to earth in order to learn new lessons for the benefit of their eternal soul – does not mean that the people we are missing so terribly will be lost to us. We are eternal beings and the people we love will be with us for eternity. There is never any rush for a person to return to earth – it may take hundreds of years – and when we are reborn, we can be reborn at the same time as the people we have loved in our previous life or lives. And when this happens, we may take on the same or a different role with that particular person so that we can learn from each other once again. Likewise, when we have died and are in the spirit world, we can be reconnected to our loved ones, and while living with and loving them once again, we can experience all the wonderful things that the spiritual realm has to offer.

I hope, then, that as people read on they will not be disturbed by the thought of reincarnation.

There were only two bedrooms upstairs in our house at that time, one for my mum and dad and the other for my sister, so I slept in a little room downstairs. One night, I found myself sitting up in bed in my tiny room, and when I next looked I saw my body lying beside me, fast asleep.

At this time, I had been involved in spiritual matters for about a year and had heard much talk about out-of-body experiences. I could hardly believe this was happening to me, though, and I was very excited. As I gazed at my body, however, a doubt crept in and I found myself wondering whether I was actually dreaming. To settle my mind, I decided to get out of the bed and have another look, and as I did so I felt something too powerful to resist drawing me out of the room, into the hall.

Directly opposite my bedroom door were the stairs, and there, to my amazement, was an orange glow. As I was reeling from the shock of this, I noticed something else. There, enveloped in the centre of the orange glow and sitting cross-legged on the top stair, was a little boy aged about fourteen. He had a shaved head and was dressed in saffron robes. As I looked at him, his facial features became clearer and I knew instantly that he was Tibetan. He was very beautiful, and there was a glow of light hovering all around him.

I was astonished, but not at all afraid. He didn't speak, just put out a hand to welcome me and indicated that I should sit in front of him. Even close up to him, I had no fear. I was happy just to sit at his feet and was unperturbed by the silence that preceded his first speaking to me. His opening words, however, have remained clearly embedded in my mind.

'You now live a life of comparative luxury,' he said softly, 'but this has not always been the case.'

With that, he showed me a simple wooden bowl which had in it a little oatmeal, a porridge-type substance, a heart-shaped leaf and something that, to this day, I can't quite put a name to. This, he was conveying to me, was what I had existed on in another, less fortunate life.

He then went on to tell me that I had once lived in Tibet, which was where he had first met and known me, and he told me of the places we had visited and many other wonderful things. Chief among these was a message that I was delighted to receive and that set my heart racing.

'You were,' he said, 'born to be different, born to pass on messages, and although your path through life may not always be easy, it is very much hoped by the spirit people that you will do as you are told and pass on the messages that they bring.'

'Oh, yes – *yes*,' I replied.

It was like one of those moments so often mentioned in the Bible when some mortal has received a heavenly visitation or heard their name called.

The next thing I knew I was back in my bed, feeling completely exhilarated, and having located a pencil and paper, I wrote down the details of what had happened.

This experience sounds mundane whenever I speak of it but it has lived with me ever since that night, and whenever I remember that Tibetan boy I feel elated, totally affirmed in the work I am doing.

The meeting with the boy was momentous, but my next meeting with a spirit was even more so.

When I was eighteen I used to sit with Marcia Ford, a trance medium, who taught me a lot. Each week when there was just the two of us in a spacious, candlelit room in her home, she would go into trance and her guide, the spirit of a deceased Buddhist monk, would come through and speak directly to me. His name was Ta Po and he was always so friendly, I knew we were mates.

Sitting quietly in her armchair, Marcia would close her eyes and soon her head would drop and Ta Po would come in. With her eyes still shut, she would then speak in the voice of Ta Po and he and I would talk for an hour or so. I could tell him anything – he really was a good friend.

During one of these trance sessions, some very important information came through.

'Your spirit guide is here,' he said. 'His name is Zintar.'

Zintar, I was told, was a ninety-two-year-old Tibetan monk when he passed from this world, and information was then given to me that I knew to be true because I had had various dreams, visions and glimpses of the two of us together in the past.

'My God,' I thought, 'this is *the* man. This is Zintar, my spirit guide.'

During that session Ta Po went on to describe the life that Zintar and I had once shared when I was a child living in Tibet. He also told me how that life had ended. Zintar and I had died together on a mountain path in an avalanche.

All this again confirmed things that I had previously glimpsed in short, tantalising visions.

As soon as Ta Po introduced Zintar as my spirit guide, I felt at one with him, and I knew that he was going to be my principal guide in this lifetime, who would always be there for me and who I could call upon for help when I was receiving messages from other people's loved ones.

That first occasion at Marcia's was a totally mind blowing experience. On that particular night, Zintar didn't come through to me directly, only through Ta Po, but a little while after this I heard him say his name and he then spoke to me in a language that I had never heard in this lifetime, but which I knew to be Tibetan.

To this day, he speaks through me when I am in trance, and works with me when I am demonstrating mediumship.

When I was still eighteen, one of the elders in the Spiritualist church, a lady who was a brilliant organiser and whose words carried much weight in the church, came up to me one night and told me that, over the past few weeks, she had been listening to the messages I had received from various mediums.

'It just so happens,' she said, 'that there is a vacancy in our home-development circle – and I'm wondering if you would like to join us.'

Now, you do not get vacancies just like *that* in home-development circles – somebody practically has to die first – and I knew that everyone who attended the meetings at the church wanted to be in that circle. I could hardly believe that she had decided to ask me.

'How old are you?' she queried as I stood there, momentarily tongue tied.

'Just eighteen,' I replied.

'That's good,' she said. 'We wouldn't have taken you if you were under eighteen.'

Walking home that night, the wind and rain in my face, I couldn't believe my luck. It seemed to be yet another confirmation that what I was intent upon doing with my life was meant to be.

The home circle was held in a semi-detached, council house rented by a very old, dapper gentleman called Harry. It was like entering a time-warp; although it was squeaky clean, nothing had been done or changed in that house since the Second World War.

Before the meetings, the six of us would sit in Harry's house having a cup of tea. Then, at seven-thirty prompt – you were not allowed in if you were late – we would go up the creaky stairs to a small back room. The walls and ceiling of the room were painted dark purple, the floor was bare wooden boards, and there was a rickety old table ringed by equally rickety chairs. Even the lampshade that hung so low its fringes brushed the table, was a dark purple. It was like a scene from a Hammer horror movie!

Once we had all managed to seat ourselves in the dark, the medium would light a candle and place it on the middle of the table. As parts of the room drifted into view that first night, I very nearly died. In the flickering candlelight, I could see eyes watching me everywhere. These eyes, I then realised, belonged to seven huge oil paintings hanging on the walls, but even when I looked away, the eyes somehow seemed to remain on me. It was like something from a Harry Potter film! These people, I was told, were the spirit guides of an old medium called Rosa Parvini. There was a young, black African man who had very kind eyes, a young German sailor, a Native American Indian who was wearing a headdress of black-and-white feathers, an Egyptian man with a headdress very much like that worn by Tutankhamen, an Egyptian woman with a magnificent gold necklace, a very old English man with long, straggly hair and a grey beard, and a fair-haired English woman.

Psychic mediums had obviously drawn on the energies from these pictures for many years, and now, convinced that the spirit world was looking at me through the paintings, I was absolutely petrified and wanted to run away as fast as my legs would carry me.

I may well have done just that if, at the moment, the medium had not begun to lead us in prayer. She then gave us hymn sheets so that we could sing a hymn called 'Open My Eyes', and as the last notes of this died away, she said, 'Close your eyes – meditate – and see what you see.'

Grateful for the opportunity to release myself from the gaze of the paintings, I closed my eyes and kept them firmly shut. For a few moments there was nothing but blackness, then I saw an image.

It was a blue human eye that floated into my mind, then went away again, followed by another, then another. My heart was sprinting and my hands were trembling. In all, I saw three blue eyes, followed very abruptly by a big green eye that seemed to be reaching into the very depths of my soul.

By the time the medium finished the session, I had worked myself into quite a state. She then spoke to each person in the group, asking what they had seen. Some spoke of pyramids, lanterns, spirit guides and feeling inspired. When she got to me, still trembling from my experience, I said, 'I didn't get anything.'

'I think you did,' she said. 'Tell me what you saw.'

'Three blue eyes, then a big green eye.'

'That's *marvellous*,' she said. 'That's the spirit people coming to have a good look at you and to welcome you into the circle.'

For a moment that made it all worse, because I was unnerved by the thought that they were watching me, sifting through my very being, and I was afraid I would be found unworthy. The next moment, though, I realised that I needed to trust that however many flaws I had, these could be worked through with the spirits' help and I could continue developing.

When I was eighteen, we moved to a much larger, detached house. By this time I had been sitting in the circle for a while, and the medium had told me that my parents were going to move house even before they mentioned it to Lorraine and me. She even described the bedroom I would have in the new house.

'When you enter your room,' she said, 'there will be a mahogany wardrobe on the right-hand side, and the room, which is a very sunny room, will have large windows that look out on to a small garden that will have a pond.'

As it happened, the house didn't have a pond when we moved in, but within three weeks, without my having said a word, Dad had put one in!

I know it was only a bedroom that the medium described so accurately, but it was a big bright space, painted white, in which I decided to create an absolutely pristine sanctuary. Unusually for a boy, I cleaned its surfaces almost every other day, always made my bed, changed its sheets and pillowcases myself, and kept its windows and skirting boards clean. All this cleanliness, I felt, was important for somebody who wanted to follow a spiritual path, and I was very disciplined about making my room into a welcoming space for any spirit who wished to visit me.

'If somebody comes from that beautiful, heavenly realm,' I told myself, 'they won't want to find yesterday's pants on the floor or grubby sheets or empty cups, bottles and cans everywhere!'

I also filled the room with candles and incense, which I lit and burned whenever I was in there. I wasn't really going over the top, it just helped me to focus on what I was doing, what I wanted from life.

While my friends were speeding up and down the Southend Road on their motorbikes, I was attending Spiritualist meetings; and while they were playing the Top Forty full blast, I was listening to meditation tapes. When they came to my house and visited my room, though, they never made me feel I was a weirdo or criticised me. They might have given it a few sidelong glances, but they were my friends. They knew I was quirky, and they just took it all in their stride, thought that was me and left me to get on with it. I never talked much about what was going on in my world, but this was not because they were judgemental. I just accepted that we were very different people who had very different interests, and that there was room in the world for all of us. As Gandalf says in *The Fellowship of the Rings*, 'All we have to do is decide what to do with the time that is given to us.'

I went to that circle in Harry's house every week for nearly two years and I learned a lot about the path I had embarked upon. Then, when I was nearly twenty years old, the lady who had first invited me to join the circle asked me and two other people if we would take the evening service in the Red Cross hall on New Year's Day.

I was very honoured, but I was so nervous that evening when I stood up to give a message that I nearly fainted, and my knee caps as well as my legs were knocking and shaking! There was a young guy present that night and I remember saying, 'I'm *very* nervous, but can I speak to you?' I then told him that I had a lady standing beside me, and having pleaded with the spirits to tell me something, I heard a name spoken.

'I've just heard the name Rose,' I said to him.

'My mum was called Rose,' he replied, 'and she is dead.'

That gave my confidence a tremendous boost and, putting my own fears to one side, I gave three messages to three different people that night. I think the initial contact was a blessing from the spirit world intended give me encouragement – and it did.

On another day, not long after, I was asked to take a service at St Matthew's Spiritualist Church, Southend-on-Sea. A beautiful old church, with pews, aisles and a proper stage made out of a rich dark wood, it was custom built for Spiritualists.

On this occasion, I had to give a fifteen-minute talk and I decided my subject would be a pioneering medium called Mrs Gunning, who had worked for some years in nearby Leigh on Sea. I never knew Mrs Gunning, but I had heard a lot of stories about her, and I knew she was called the 'flowers and fruit medium' because when she was conducting a séance in a darkened room, the spirits would walk around bringing gifts of fresh flowers and fruit.

The story I told the congregation was given to me by a wonderful old man called Alan Crosley who was actually present at one of her séances. When Alan was a young man during the Second World War, he had sat with Mrs Gunning at a time when food was rationed and people couldn't get a banana for love nor money. During the course of this séance, the spirit people had said, 'We are bringing gifts', and when the lights were turned on, the room was full of fruit and flowers – bananas, pineapples, oranges and peaches. Although people who sat with Mrs Gunning were quite used to such events, they were still amazed at the sheer abundance of the gifts and they took most of the flowers and fruit to local hospitals.

As I was relaying this experience to my audience of about thirty people, I had just got to the point of talking about the

flowers and fruit when there was a sudden ripple of disturbance in the congregation.

'Oh my God, are my flies undone?' was my first red-faced
thought, followed by: 'Is something happening behind me?'

It was a major disturbance, and I didn't have the experience
then to remain cool and simply ask what was going on. But the
next moment, as I glanced over my shoulder, I could see that
the bouquet of fresh flowers on the table behind me was
shaking and vibrating.

It emerged that the congregation had first noticed this when
I got to the point of saying 'the flowers and fruit medium', and
that, having vibrated, one of the long-stemmed flowers had
been lifted about twelve inches from the vase and had hovered
there for a moment before being returned to the vase, then
levitated again. Meanwhile, the other flowers in the vase had
gently shook and it was this that I had caught the tail end of.

It was such an amazing experience that I finished my talk by
saying, 'I am sure Mrs Gunning thoroughly approves of being
remembered here tonight, and the flowers moving were manifesting her approval.'

In my view, this event illustrates how clever spirits can be;
and for some of the people present that night, who were
unsure as to whether or not they believed in the spirit world,
it was a life-changing experience.

I also used to work at the Spiritualist church as a pro-
bationary healer – a person who uses their hands to channel
the healing energy of the Great Spirit into another person. Lots
of people used to queue up for me, but there was one guy who
insisted on seeing me every Sunday, week in, week out. This
man, who had been to many different doctors, including
Harley Street specialists, was having nosebleeds all the time,
and by the time he came to me, the medical profession had
basically given up on him.

Cupping my hands around his nose, I would pray that I could be a useful channel for healing and that something wonderful would happen and he would be cured. During these times, my hands would get very shaky and hot, and I would feel an extraordinary energy flowing through them. I would do that for fifteen minutes and saw him for six weeks in all. At the end of this time, something wonderful – miraculous – *did* happen. The bleeding stopped and did not return.

I cannot begin to say how delighted I was for him. As for me, I found it a very humbling experience because I knew I could not have achieved that healing without the help of my spirit friends.

I also gave healing to a lady who was unable to eat food and who had to exist on a liquid diet because she couldn't swallow. A lot of her problems were thought to be psychological. Her father had died and she had been left feeling dreadful because she felt she had failed him and wasn't worthy of any good experiences. By the time I saw her, she had had countless operations and she kept telling me not to touch her throat. One day, the spirits moved me to ignore this instruction and I centred the healing on her throat. She went berserk, telling me she didn't deserve to eat, didn't want to be healed. She *wanted* to be punished. But the spirits had other ideas; they wanted to heal her, and she was healed.

I can only confirm what is true: God – the Great Spirit, the Creator, call this force what you will – 'works in wondrous ways his/her wonders to perform'.

Whenever I talk about what some of us call God, and others the Great Spirit, the Creator, the ultimate force that breathes life into all of us, the eternal energy of the universe, I personally think of this Creator as a *she* rather than a *he*. To me, our Creator is more she than he because I think of the Creator as a motherly, nurturing, creative force. In truth, though, I am sure our Creator is androgynous!

Likewise, although – then and now – I often work as a medium in Spiritualist churches, I never pigeon-hole myself as just a Spiritualist, as I also embrace parts of other religions, along with the wonderful teachings and philosophies Spiritualism has to offer. Labels can be divisive and I do not want to limit myself to any one faith or belief structure. I never pretend to be other than I am. I simply describe myself as a medium, who is blessed with the ability to see, hear and feel things very clearly at times, and somebody who is, therefore, able to bring comfort to the relatives and friends of the dead.

When I first started serving the churches, the 'services' were usually held in battered halls or in rooms above shops, but I rather liked that – and still do, to a degree.

On one such Sunday – a freezing cold day when the wind was biting the features off my face – I remember travelling to a 'church' in Walthamstow in the east end of London to do a service. When I arrived at this tiny, purpose-built Spiritualist church, a man showed me into the medium's room which was behind the rostrum and so small that I swear if I'd been fatter I wouldn't have fitted in. It really was tiny, with only enough space for a chair, and when the door closed in my face I swear to God that it was so cold in there that I could see my own breath. After half an hour or so, shut in this freezing cold 'fridge' of a room, I was led into the church to do the demonstration to the four people in the congregation.

When I think back to that Sunday, it makes me laugh, because it was such a hideously dull, boring night. No one wanted to speak to me, they only wanted dead people to speak to them!

Yet there were so many occasions like this in the early days, when I would travel miles, give it my all, and just about get my expenses covered.

'That was nice,' members of the congregation would say as I

was preparing to make the long journey home. Then, as if they were doing me a favour, they would add: 'Yes . . . we would like you to come back again.'

'Thank you so much for giving me the opportunity,' I would reply, totally sincere.

I guess those were the years that represented my apprenticeship.

When I was twenty-one, I used to do public demonstrations of mediumship in Spiritualist churches. I was always very nervous, so one day I teamed up with my friend Marcia Ford, who was also a clairvoyant, and we did the demonstration as a duo for a while. We were like the Sonny and Cher of the church circuit.

Once, when we were driving home after one of these demonstrations, we both said how wonderful the evening had been, how much we had enjoyed it and how utterly determined we were to continue dedicating our lives to working for spirit. There and then we made a pact that we would both continue to do this for the rest of our lives.

Having dropped Marcia off at her home, I continued on my way. All through the rest of the journey I had a truly awful feeling that I was being watched by someone – something – not at all nice.

When I phoned Marcia the next day, I discovered that she had had exactly the same feeling from the minute she got out of my car.

'Why don't you come over to my house,' she said, 'so that we can try to sort this out? It might be a malicious spirit who overheard us making our pact.'

When I arrived at Marcia's house, we went up to her meditation room, which was decorated with blue wallpaper and lit by a white candle. It was a lovely, warm, sunny day, but as we sat down at the table, the room was suddenly icy cold, so cold that we could see our breath around us. Then the candle started to spit as if somebody was sprinkling water on it, then it began to blow large smoke-rings and the flame bounced off the top of the candle and started to slide slowly down its side before travelling back to the top again. How the flame managed to hop off the wick and travel down and up the side of the candle where there was no wick is inexplicable. There was also a horrible, sickly feeling in the room, and it was altogether a very unnerving experience.

'Don't worry,' Marcia said, 'this is what we are going to do.' And, indicating that I should do what she did, she started to chant in a loud, clear voice.

'Into the light, into love,' we both chanted several times. 'Light is greater than darkness, courage is greater than fear. We banish you – you have no power over us. We are going to work with the spirit world whether you like it or not.'

A few moments later, the room returned to a normal temperature and the sickly feeling that had hovered all around us went too. The malignant spirit had obviously withdrawn.

Later, Marcia and I decided that, having dedicated our lives to the spirits, we were on probation, being tested by the spirit world to see how we would cope with any negative forces and whether we would be scared off by them. Perhaps the fact that we were not afraid and had remained true to our resolve and dedication meant that we had passed an initiation test; that they now knew that when we came across difficult, negative things we would overcome them.

Since I started work as a medium, people have often asked me if I believe in evil spirits, and I always reply: 'There's light, there's dark, there's good, there's bad in all people in this world, and the same applies to spirits and the spirit world.' Just as there are misguided, malevolent people, there are misguided, malevolent spirits who we need to be mindful of. As a medium, I want to concentrate on letting people know that all is love and light, good, fabulous and fantastic, but I know there is a tiny number of misguided spirits who are still within reach of the earth and who haven't seen the error of their ways.

Personally, I believe in natural law, and natural law dictates that 'like attracts like'. If you are a good, loving and honest human, you will attract good, loving spirit people. If you are mean spirited, you will attract that kind of energy around you. This 'like to like' can be seen working in everyday life. Happy, fun-loving, outgoing people attract friends of a similar ilk. Criminals hang around with other criminals, drug addicts hang out with drug addicts. This is the way that natural law works. Likewise, people who practise what is known as the dark arts tune in to that level. We are rather like radio receivers. If we choose to tune in to dark forces, we will find them.

I have never doubted the course I set my heart upon. By the time I was twenty-two, I had read every spiritual book I could lay my hands upon and I still wanted to learn more. By then, most of my schoolfriends were engaged or married, but I was still unattached and living at home with my parents. There were times, though, when I found myself wishing that I had someone in my life who would share my interest in the paranormal and with whom I could discuss everything under the sun.

The spirits must have heard me! One night, when I was due to give a demonstration of clairvoyance in a small community hall in nearby Pitsea, Essex, this hope was realised.

4
Time Past, Time Present

The evening was going well. Feeling confident and receptive, I had just received several significant messages from people's loved ones, and there was a general air of contentment in the small community hall in Pitsea.

As I was stepping off the small raised platform to join in the tea break with the twenty or so people present, a young guy caught my eye. I wasn't in the habit of singling out people on these occasions, but I was immediately drawn to him. He looked different from the usual members who attended the meetings.

During the interval, shy though I usually am, I stood next to him while I was drinking my cup of tea. His name, he told me, was Stuart and he was an Essex boy who lived locally. The conversation that followed was so in line with my own beliefs on spiritual matters that it left me hoping that our paths would cross again soon.

The following week, this man kept coming to mind. So, on the Thursday, although I was not booked to take the meeting that night, I decided I would go back to the community hall in Pitsea as an observer.

I saw Stuart and sat next to him. Once again, I found myself drawn to talk to him while we were having a cup of tea in the interval. During that conversation, it became even more obvious that, like me, he was a person on a spiritual quest. Then, as it became clear that he was looking for a development group to join, and as by then I had one of my own, I invited him along to my group.

'*Really?*' he said, delighted, 'I'd love to come.'

Development groups vary in size from two people upwards, but mostly they are about ten or so strong. A distinction has to be made between these and the old-fashioned circles that were so named because the members always sat in a circle! In the latter there were usually between six and eight people and a medium. People didn't speak about meditation in those days – it was called 'linking in' – and it was a period when members closed their eyes and just allowed spirits to drop thoughts into their minds. Then the medium would look around and say something like, 'So-and-so is here with us today.' These meetings were very much geared around your spirit guides and what they wanted to say, and they could manifest in one form or another in the room, by transplanting their features on the medium's face, or by talking through the medium in trance.

Such circles were always very hard to come by because they required total dedication. People would sit in the same circle every week for years and never miss a meeting. It was very disciplined. I remember reading a book about a medium who had two male sitters who, even when they went on holiday (fortunately they didn't go abroad very often in those days), would travel back to sit with the circle and then return to their holiday destination. They regarded being in a circle as having made an appointment with the spirit world, and that appointment would not be broken unless they had a major illness or died.

These days, circles that require that level of dedication are not so common and they are more often called development groups. Essentially these are workshops, and people can pick and choose from a number that they might want to attend in any one year. I now take five development groups a month: four in the College of Psychic Studies in South Kensington, the other in Wickford, Essex. I usually give the students a subject title, such as Séance Work or Working with your Spirit Guide, then I create workshop exercises for that subject.

Basically, I lead twenty or so people at a time through the various aspects of a paranormal workshop. Television, radio and magazines have brought psychic words into everyday usage, but students who come to development groups want to study what a medium and mediumship is in greater depth. They also want to learn about the difference between *physical* and *mental* mediumship, clairvoyance, clairaudience, clairsentience, and what it means to be truly psychic.

In my groups, I also teach meditation, how to breathe, how to become more aware of spirit people, how to practise giving clairvoyance to each other, and how to recognise when the spirits are in the room. Really, the classes are all about enabling those who are interested to be more receptive to their own psychic powers. We all have these and it is a question of teaching students how to connect with them and develop their gifts. Some people attend because they are interested in becoming a medium; others come just out of interest and end up becoming brilliant mediums! Some are led there by an inner voice and attending the development group completely changes the direction of their life.

Without a doubt, we are now seeing more and more young people turning from the norm, so to speak, and giving a portion of their day or week to spiritual matters, to questioning what life is all about and what happens next. These are questions which most of us ask at one time or another when we realise that there is more to life than materialism.

When a person starts meditating and opening up to the universe, what they are doing, in effect, is getting a sense of true reality. Reality is not as we habitually see it; true reality is appreciating that we are from the spirit world, and that we are reborn into the physical world, invariably to be with people we have known before in previous lives. We then have another opportunity to live our life the best way we can, and when that mission is hopefully accomplished we journey back to the spirit world again.

Over the next six months Stuart never missed one of my evening development groups and, slowly, we became good mates who discussed everything under the sun. We truly were soul mates. Our interests in the paranormal complemented each other, and we just never ran out of conversation and ideas to discuss relating to the spirit world and life after physical death.

Although he was a gifted psychic himself, who was strongly drawn to the paranormal, Stuart chose not to become a medium, but to dedicate his time to a career in publishing instead. He still took up every opportunity, though, to study anything to do with psychic matters. And once we had met we discovered time and time again that we were seeking answers to the same questions, and the two of us would sit around for hours discussing all manner of things, from past lives to the reasons for our being here.

'When I was five years of age,' I remember telling him, 'I had this recurring memory of me as a young Egyptian boy named Yem, lying on a cold slab while women dressed in long black robes were washing me, tending me, looking after me. I was totally paralysed, unable to move or speak. And, would you believe it, some years later when I was sitting with a wonderful trance medium, I was absolutely gobsmacked when a spirit guide spoke through her and told me that I had once lived a life in Egypt, where I had been slowly poisoned by an ambitious uncle to the point where I had become totally paralysed. That was amazing – *awesome*.'

When I was twenty-one, I had felt the need to be regressed by hypnosis to this incarnation, and under the hypnotist's instructions I'd gone straight back to this life in Egypt. First, I had found myself in an opulent place, with huge columns running around the sides of a big marble hall that was lit by pottery oil lamps. Next, I was being chased by a swarthy-faced man in white flowing robes, then I was caught and forced to drink some poison from a small glass vial. The whole murderous deed was laid out in front of me and I became so distressed that the hypnotist asked me what was happening.

'I can't move my arms or legs,' I cried out, distraught. 'I can't see and can hardly breath my throat is tightening.'

'Take yourself back to the time you died,' he said. 'How old were you then?'

'Seventeen,' I replied.

'Take yourself back to the death experience.'

When I did what I was told, I felt my spirit being lifted out of my body, then my spirit was free and I was looking down at a beautiful, young Egyptian boy, laid out on a slab, who I knew was me.

'Take yourself forward,' the hypnotist said.

And I did. This is how I know what it's like to die. There was this shimmering, pearl-like light all around me and I was weightless, free, floating in the sky. Then I entered a dazzling light and there was an Egyptian woman waiting there who came to me, her arms open. Her hair was plaited in magnificent braids and she had rings on her fingers and toes and was wearing a pure white tunic that dazzled my eyes.

'Mother,' I remember greeting her, but she wasn't the mother I have now in this life. She was my mother *then*, and I was somehow completely aware that she had died when I was a baby and that she now had her arms outstretched to greet me.

'Come,' she said, and, totally unafraid, I went to her. She then took me by the hand and led me away.

It was an amazing experience, one that revealed to me what happens to us in the moment of dying.

Some years later, on a three-week holiday to Egypt, I went to visit the Karnak temple complex at Thebes, which sprawls across much of northern Luxor. The pylons and sandstone pillars of the massive Temple of Amun loom over the ruins of the smaller chapels that are scattered throughout the enclosure. The day had started perfectly normally and I was fine when I arrived, but after a while I began to experience a feeling of total panic and I could not wait to get out of the place. I could not explain why I was rendered so frantic in that particular spot, but it was a very uncomfortable experience – one that I have no wish to repeat. All I knew then – and now – was that the panic had something to do with a past life I had lived in Egypt.

While there, I also went to another temple, which was embedded in rock and situated in a dry, arid area. Apart from the temple itself, there was nothing there. But as I stood by the entrance, the area around me was suddenly transformed. The dryness of the earth disappeared and was replaced by a lush, green oasis that was full of palm trees, with little streams and the sound of trickling water. There was a wonderful perfume of incense and exotic flowers wafting all around me. There was also a sense of ancient Egyptians going about their daily work, carrying wonderful trays of fruit and vegetables that were about to be prepared in the kitchens. The whole scene was very dramatic and vivid, and I was totally transfixed by the vision.

Later, when I was talking to the tour guide, he said, 'When this temple was built, this place was an oasis.'

'Oh my God!' I thought. 'Just a few minutes ago, my mind flipped back to how this place would have looked thousands of years ago.'

In those early days of knowing Stuart, I also told him about the incarnation that I had had as a child in Tibet – the one in which I had shared a life with my spirit guide, Zintar. I was about eight or nine and Zintar was old and bent and walked with the aid of a staff. The vision, which I had many glimpses of as a child, was so clear that I knew the pen-and-ink outline of the mountains etched against the blue sky, and the weather was so bitterly cold and gusty that I was following him with my head bent down. Suddenly, hearing a sound like water rushing over rapids, I looked up and there was this great avalanche, with huge boulders coming down. Then I was struck and I remembered no more.

I also have some powerful memories of three unhappy, tormented lives that followed each other. In two of these, I experienced the pain and horror of being at the receiving end of terrible beatings; in the other I was the tyrant doing the beating, with a leather-thonged whip in my hand. The most vivid of these flashbacks featured me as a black slave, manacled by leg irons and being taken further and further away from my homeland on a ship that had huge billowing sails. I was in a rat-infested hold, suffering the mental anguish and physical agonies of a slave who had just left a brilliantly sunny place for this black hole.

I believe my last life, the one before this one, was a life lived in Bournemouth, which seems terribly mundane after Egypt, Tibet and slave ships. I remember catching glimpses of this when I was a schoolchild. These came in the form of flashbacks of me as a handsome young man of about twenty years old. I had flattened Brylcreemed hair and I was working as an entertainer in an old-time music hall from about 1910 to 1915. The visions for this particular life often included a pier and other seaside scenes, when life seemed to be full of happy, carefree days peopled by bright young things and dapper-looking gentlemen. It was all very flamboyant.

When I actually went to Bournemouth recently, I was in for a few surprises. I knew what was around one particular bend in a street even before I'd driven round it. I knew there would be a wonderful tea-room at the bottom and there was. I'd never been to this place in this lifetime, but I had a vivid memory of being in there before and somebody pouring me a cup of tea from a blue-and-white striped teapot.

This reminds me of a recent incident. A few weeks ago I was at a party at my friend Alison's house, and as usual I was one of the last to leave. By this stage, the few of us who were left were dancing to the swing music of the Rat Pack. As I was dancing with Alison, I suddenly found myself transported back to the 1920s, to the days when people danced the Charleston. The strange thing was that Alison and I were there together, dressed in 1920s clothes and dancing with one another. Although I was calling my dancing partner 'Daphne' in this vision, I had absolutely no doubt that it was Alison. Her face was exactly the same, but, dare I say it, she was slimmer and had a typical period bobbed hairstyle.

I knew then that I had known Alison in a past life, that her name then was Daphne and mine was Archie. I am *so* glad we have reconnected in this life and that we are once again really good friends who enjoy dancing together!

Whenever I talk to friends about my past lives, I know I am not just being fanciful or making up stories to impress them. They are vivid flashbacks – true memories – which flow back into my consciousness. Far from feeling troubled, I feel blessed that I am able to have these glimpses of my previous incarnations. While they show that I have the potential to be a bastard as well as a good person, I know that each of these lives has given me the opportunity to live out karma – my fate, my destiny that is determined by the sum of all my past deeds, good and bad, in any one lifetime – and continue to develop. This, in my view, is what each life is for, another opportunity to use the allotted timespan we are given to earn good or bad karma, which then determines the circumstances we are born into for our next life.

'How can you be sure that these memories of your various incarnations are not dreams?' a friend asked me one evening.

'I can only say that I experience memories, flashbacks and dreams in very different ways,' I replied. 'Dreams – the kind we all have when we are asleep – are often full of random, nonsensical images. But memories and flashbacks of previous lives are not just visual, they engage all the senses. I can smell and hear them as well as see them and I even know what certain things feel and taste like. They open up like a three-dimensional book, and when I go back and relive this or that particular tableau, they are as real as the moment I am living right now. And I have most of these flashbacks when I am awake.'

I believe that many people can remember certain episodes from their past lives, and can sense that they may have met a particular person or been in a particular place before. Certain memories and flashbacks can pop into our subconscious or be given to us as visions from our spirit guides. I don't necessarily know *why* I have any one particular memory, but I do know they have a purpose; that at some level they are necessary, helpful to me as benchmarks, dividers in the life that I am living now. One life is like one chapter in a book, but life, like a book, has many chapters!

I know some people believe their dreams are meaningful and love to interpret them, but I have no desire to investigate dreams further. This does not mean that I do not believe they can be great sources of inspiration and guidance. It is simply that they are not my thing at this moment in time.

What I find much more interesting is how clearly a spirit can be with us even when we are in a sleeping state. On one occasion, for example, I wasn't aware of coming out of my body, but I found myself wide awake, having an out-of-body experience and watching myself walking along a motorway with my sister.

'Oh!' I remember thinking. 'I'm out of my body. Is Lorraine OK? I can't believe she's made it out of her body, too – that's incredible.'

'Come with me,' I said, holding her firmly by the hand.

I didn't feel afraid, but I was puzzled, apprehensive, wondering why I was on a motorway. Then, as we walked down the deserted carriageway, I suddenly saw a dark, twisted shape ahead of us. Coming closer, I could see that it was the metal of a silver-grey car that had crashed and was lying, its wheels still turning, on its side on the hard shoulder. There were no other cars on the road, but this car, a tangled mass of metal, was a total wreck, a write-off. As I inspected it more closely and peered through the broken driver's window, I was in for a shock. Inside was a young guy, dying from his injuries. Somehow, having succeeded in contorting and compacting my own body, I managed to lower myself and my sister into the car.

The man was in far too serious a condition to hear me, but I knew he was conscious of my presence and I kept on speaking words of comfort to him. All of a sudden, I realised my sister was no longer beside me, but there was no time to be distracted by this because I was now using all my strength to ease the man from the car. As I continued in my attempts to pull his trapped, broken body out of the driver's seat, I realised

tragedy, and who have never before spoken in a public arena, have come to the fore and set up action or support groups that are helping countless others.

In my work, I have experienced suicides, car crash and murder victims coming to me from the spirit world. Although I know from their messages that not everyone is happy at first to find themselves in the spirit world, I also know that the potential for healing is there. Often it really is just a matter of time before the other spirits coax them back to a sense of happiness.

I had confirmation of how such a spirit can be healed when I was doing a one-to-one reading in Denmark. A young girl who had been brutally murdered came through for a member of her family, and there was nothing but an absolute sense of well-being in the room.

'I'm fine now,' she said. 'It's all over and done with. I'm very happy in the spirit world.'

Acceptance, of course, can be even harder for loved ones who are left behind. Sudden deaths are very hard to come to terms with because there is no 'cushion' to prepare you and let you down slowly.

I used to read a lot for a woman who had lost her son, Simon, when he was run over while crossing the road.

'Tell my mum I'm all right,' he would say time and time again when he came through, but his mother was rendered so low by her grief that she couldn't possibly accept his messages.

When somebody commits suicide, people sometimes believe that they go to purgatory and are left to suffer in a no man's land. Yet I have had people coming through who have committed suicide, and I have no sense that they are suffering at all. I feel their situation is no different from any other person who has died; if anything, they are shocked to discover that they cannot die, that life is eternal.

Knowing what I now know, I would urge people who are suffering from depression and feeling suicidal to go on with their life and seek help for their depression. But if the person has already gone, we can only embrace the fact that they are now in the spirit world, free from their pain, and receiving healing. Above all, I would want anyone who feels they have lost a loved one to suicide to know that the person is not being punished and made to suffer even more in purgatory. The God – the Great Spirit – that I believe in is a loving, forgiving God, and that is not how She works!

My ideal way of dying would be for all the people I love most in this world to go before me! This is because I would hate to be left worrying, while I was dying, about how they would manage emotionally and healthwise, or cope with being lonely without me. I don't want the people around me to suffer. I would rather take that pain on for them and endure the grief of their loss than be left knowing that they would have to grieve for and do without me in the world. Knowing that they are going to a better place – a beautiful place – helps me in this, of course.

As for my own death, I would like to die knowing that I have been successful in my work and that I have left a trail of good things behind me. I would like to be in a warm bed with crisp, white sheets, listening to a spirit voice that is saying, 'You've done well, Tony. Go to sleep now and you will be with us soon.' I would then like to drift into sleep and become aware, as my spirit leaves my body and enters the light, that I've got a young spirit body again and that my family and loved ones who have already passed are there to greet me. That would be a perfect way to die!

Certainly, given my experiences in this life, I have no fear of death. At some level I am actually looking forward to it and I get quite excited when I think about it. Like most people, though, I fear the method of despatch, but I know the actual passing over is going to be a wonderful, joyous release, when all struggle and strife and being tugged by this or that desire will be over. All that will be necessary then in order to return to that creative source – which I have already experienced as a nurturing, loving and totally harmonious being – is the giving up, the surrendering of this lifetime.

Whenever people ask me if I am *really* so confident that there is life after death, I say, 'Yes, because thanks to Zintar, I have experienced it.'

This, my most powerful out-of-body experience, took place when I was twenty-six. Once again I woke up, out of my body, and it was an incredible feeling because I was actually in the spirit world. Before, when I had had out-of-body experiences, I had found myself in the house or on a motorway, but this time I was in the spirit world and it was fabulous – mind blowing.

I saw myself standing with Zintar in the spirit world, on a snow-covered mountain peak, looking out at all the other mountains surrounding me, all with the same snow-covered peaks. It was a barren but totally alive landscape and the sky was the colour of lilac, an indigo sky, and just the most beautiful thing I had ever seen. The clouds were a soft, pale, light grey, and the feeling I had was like being wrapped in a duvet filled with love.

'Zintar,' I said, '*please* don't send me back. As much as I love my family, my friends and my dog, I *don't* want to go back. I *don't* want to leave this place.'

'Tony,' he replied, 'you have to go back to continue the work, but I have brought you to this place, at this time, to show you what awaits you.'

After he left me and I woke up, I cried on and off for three days. I was a totally fit, healthy, happy young man, but I didn't want to be back on earth. I can only describe that experience as a sense of total oneness with everything good, a sense of being totally accepted, held and loved. There was no struggle, just perfection.

I am now aware that there are many different aspects of the spirit world, but that experience was my little bit of heaven. Going to the spirit world was such a blessing, not least because I now know that I have nothing to fear from my personal passing. It will be wonderful, and I will see my granddads, nans, Aunt Grace, and anybody else who has passed over before me. I am obviously concerned that I may have to go through illness, suffering and pain first, but I'll face that if I need to in order to get there.

Once when Zintar spoke through me when I was in a trance, the group sitting with me asked, 'Zintar, where are you speaking from in the spirit world?'

When I heard his answer on a taped recording after the seance, it made me shiver.

'I am speaking to you from the Land of the Indigo Sky,' he said. 'I am with other spirits who live in this land. We are spirit incarnations of Tibetan Buddhist monks.'

It was almost as if that group of spirits, who lived in that glorious place, had chosen to be my guides, and I was a part of that group soul, that group energy, that little bit of heaven that they call the Land of the Indigo Sky.

When I am in a trance, I feel that I turn away from myself, move to one side, so that the spirit's energy can blend with my energy and can speak words through my mouth. The spirits use my vocal chords, but they have different intonations and accents. The weirdest thing is that they sometimes speak in a language that I have no knowledge of, but which I think is an ancient form of Hebrew and at other times Tibetan. Whatever it is, I know it is a blessing to be able to hear it. The words may be beyond my comprehension, but I sense they are spiritual chants that contain a blessing for all who hear them.

Some years ago, when I was in a development group for psychics, I heard Zintar saying, 'These are words that we once spoke together.' I didn't understand the meaning of the ancient guttural-sounding sentences I then heard, but I wept after that experience. I was just so touched that he had taken the trouble to come that close to me to speak in a language we had once shared. I believe I have known Zintar for many aeons and that he is my oldest friend. I regard it as a great blessing – and absolutely amazing – that he comes through to assist me in my work.

I have been extremely fortunate over the years to have come across many people who have never doubted the sincerity of my beliefs. Occasionally, though, I do meet people who think I am 'a nut case'! What is important is that *I* know I am not, and when I come up against people who say, 'Come on, matey, surely you don't believe that? Pull the other one!' I make it clear that I have no wish to convince or convert them. I do care what people think, but I am happy for them to take their own time in finding and embracing spiritual matters. If they disagree with what I am saying, I just hope that, having met me, they will question *why* they disagree with me. That's a beginning!

I don't think any of us has all the answers to this life or the next, and my way is not necessarily right for everybody. I just feel that we all need to work out what we believe to be true, because then we will be much stronger as individuals and much better equipped to cope with all the crap that we have to go through. St Augustus summed this up when he said, 'For those who believe . . . no explanation is necessary. For those who do not, no explanation is possible.'

My meeting with Stuart, then, in the community hall at Pitsea, was a great blessing. I truly had a need for a friend in my life who understood my vocation and where I was coming from, and who was willing to share the highs and lows. There are, I am sure, very few people out there who would suffer the life of a medium. We are *not* normal people! We live between two worlds. There are moments when I am off in that other world, my eyes glazed over, my emotions otherwise engaged, and I need people in my life who will let me be without constantly asking why I am as I am. Such a life is not everyone's cup of tea and psychics definitely need special people around them who accept, understand and appreciate the work they are doing.

Stuart is always ready to give me advice when I need it. He thinks everything through very carefully, and sometimes I think the spirit world finds it easier to get through to him than to me!

I do many psychic readings in the course of a week, and I often come across people who tell me similar sad, tragic stories. Slowly and painfully, a woman may find the courage to murmur that she was abused when she was a child and she is now on her fourth husband, is having an affair, and is still restless and ready to move on from one relationship to another. No one, it seems, can fill the void in her that she so needs to be filled.

I always tell such people, male and female, and they don't always like it, that first we have to embrace, forgive and love ourselves; that when we can do that, we will not need to look to others to tell us how great we are. When we feel OK about ourselves it is easier for others to love us, and for us to love others and form the relationships we desire. So many relationships are brought about – or overburdened by – unfinished business in our past, or simply by sexual attraction and desire which inevitably fades in time. True, enduring relationships engage the whole being and are sustained by the compatibility of personalities, character and spirit.

Without a doubt, everybody needs someone who is their best friend and soul mate, and I have been very lucky to have so many good friends in my life, people I have met in a variety of ways, but who I am absolutely sure I was meant to meet. I met Dan seven years ago when I was on holiday with some friends. As often happens in larger groups who go away together, there was some tension and, because of this, Stuart and I decided to go out for an evening on our own. As I was standing at a bar, ordering some drinks, there was a young man next to me. The minute I saw his face I was sure that I knew him. Having talked to each other, however, it became clear that, although we lived within a twenty-minute drive of each other in Essex, we had never met. The next day, I met up with Dan and some of his friends at the beach, and as we got on so well, we spent much of the holiday together. At the end of the two weeks, Dan and I exchanged telephone numbers, and since then he has become one of my closest friends who I see every week. He is such a positive influence in my life, I am certain we were meant to meet, meant to be friends.

I have come to believe that sometimes people are drawn to a place, such as a bar, a pub, a concert, a theatre, a dinner engagement, so that they can meet someone with whom soul recognition takes place. The sense of these occasions is always: 'The first time I looked at him (or her), I *knew* that I had known him before.'

This was the case when I met another kindred spirit, my friend Carol Bohmer. She and I became the best of friends after a chance meeting over a cup of tea at a Spiritualist church hall some twelve years ago. Once we had started chatting, we were immediately drawn to each other and it was as if we had known each other forever. Later, Carol told me that when she had seen me working at a public demonstration two years previously, she had turned to the friend she was with and said, 'I don't know this man, but on some level I *do* know him. I also know that one day we will meet and become really good friends.'

I met two other close friends, Alison and Laurie, some years ago in rather amusing circumstances in a fast-food restaurant. The first thing I said to Alison, who was tucking into a huge plate of chicken and salad, and who I seemed to recognise at once, was: 'How can anybody eat *so* much?' Fate later played a part in this friendship. When I was buying a house, the one I liked best and ended up acquiring in Wickford, Essex, turned out to be only a hundred yards from one that Alison and Laurie had moved into at more or less the same time. We are now practically neighbours, and I have two wonderful dog-sitters whenever I am working away from home.

By the time I was twenty-four, I was working harder than ever at being a medium, but I never regretted taking the psychic path and having a lifestyle that was different from other people's. There was nothing I wanted to change. I regarded the work – the visions, feelings, healing, trances, teaching and demonstrations – as absolute blessings. I still had as many difficulties to go through as other people, but I felt I could cope with these more easily, because I could see them in perspective and learn from them. My attitude was: 'So what if I don't get the splendid car or the bigger house? At least I'm not trying to cut someone's throat to get myself promoted and reach the top of the ladder.' What we are and how we live, I had concluded by then, is all part of the great game plan, of playing our particular part in life's rich pageant.

By accepting myself as I was and not squandering time

worrying or wanting things to be different, I had not wasted precious hours trying to be something I was not – and that had given me the freedom to concentrate, body, heart and soul, on my vocation and my work.

5
Is There Really Life After Death?

People often come up to me and say, 'Why are the messages that come through from the spirit world so banal? Why should spirits care about Auntie Susan's favourite hairbrush or the time when Uncle Bert stubbed his big toe on a girder? Surely they've got better things than that to communicate!'

'It depends on the spirit,' I reply. 'If your uncle was a light-hearted, humorous guy when he was alive, he is not going to come through talking about politics and international affairs; he's going to remind you of the kind of man he was. And if your grandmother was a brilliant housewife, who loved to make shortcrust pastry and was famed for her sausage rolls, she's not going to come through quoting lines from *The Complete Works of William Shakespeare*; she's going to ask if you remember the sausage rolls she used to bake. This is part and parcel of how the spirits present the evidence of letting you know who they are. The messages are true to the personality of the person concerned. When we pass into the world of spirit, it is just another stage in our progression. We do not become enlightened or politically active beings over-night. We are just as we were in life, but in spirit form. We keep our personalities.'

In my experience, when someone does receive high-minded, life-changing, philosophical messages, these often come through a trance medium who is in contact with higher spiritual entities such as spirit guides, who speak directly through him or her. But for mediums connecting with the spirits of relatives who want to make contact with living loved ones, the messages are usually family-based and evidence of identity is given in simple everyday pieces of information.

Another common criticism – and one that was thrown at me by the presenter during a radio interview – is: 'How dare you claim that you are communicating with the spirits of people's loved ones when all you are doing is taking advantage of their grief. How can you make me believe you are genuine?'

The truth is that, in these circumstances, I cannot. The presenter was so opinionated, so dogmatic in her beliefs, and her mind was so set on producing a lively, controversial programme, that whatever I said would not have made an iota of difference. She was not listening, could not hear me. She had never seen me work, but had made up her mind already. I am always happy to spread the good news that we haven't lost our loved ones, that life is eternal, but it is not my lot in life to convince every person I meet. Communication is a two-way process in which each of us has to be open at least a chink or two before we can receive! Of course, I understand that some people have doubts and I never mind people questioning me. If someone says, for example, 'I really don't know what to believe, but I'm very interested to find out more,' that's fine by me. But if people come in on the attack, saying, 'I think you're a fraud – prove to me otherwise,' I reply, 'Then please collect your coat and leave right now.'

To me, that kind of approach is not a challenge. I have a waiting list of people who are in genuine need of a sitting, and I do not mind at all if one belligerent person walks in and straight out of the door. I only mind that their relatives or friends, who are in the spirit world, may have lost the opportunity of being heard.

True mediums are always conscious of people's need for evidence, and they will seek the spirit's help in getting a description and a sense of personality. If they can also get a name, that's perfect. Likewise, a sincere psychic medium giving a one-to-one reading will always try to prove that they are tuned in to the person who has come for the sitting as well as their loved ones. They may, for example, begin by mentioning simple things that the sitter has done that day, or something that she spoke about in the car on the way to the sitting. This gives evidence that her loved one's spirits were present, were listening, and have conveyed this information to the medium. This is the kind of evidence that a person who comes to a sitting should expect.

Another criticism is: 'If you are given a gift from God, you should do it for free and not charge.'

But is the gift of mediumship any different from a gift that enables you to be an artist, writer, poet, musician or doctor? Like everybody else, mediums have to eat and pay their way through everyday life!

Of course there are charlatans – cruel people – who make things up as they go along and take advantage of others when they at their most vulnerable. There are unfortunately bad apples in every field of work. The tragedy is that these people and their tricks do terrible harm by perpetuating the lie that all mediums are false and not to be trusted.

A horror I have recently come across arrives through the post: 'You have been picked at random by our sensitives,' the letter says, 'send $50 and we will predict your future.' Lonely people who want to know what the future may hold are an easy target. One man I know who responded has since had another hundred or so prediction-offer letters. When he made enquiries, he discovered he had been identified as vulnerable to such approaches and his name had been added to a database. It really is a great pity that such things exist, because good psychics, mediums and sensitives get tarred with the same brush.

In truth, I do not believe that spirits are able to predict the future as such, but I have known them to bring certain insights to their loved ones from their vantage point in the spirit world. Free from their own bodies and the tangled web of life, they are sometimes able to see things more clearly than we do, and they may suggest a wise course of action if we present them with our problems.

There are always so many different levels to take into consideration. For example, I believe that when we are re-incarnated, we are reborn with a kind of blueprint already in place which determines the kind of circumstances we will meet during our next life on earth. I also believe that because that blueprint is in place, spirits are able to advise us on certain aspects of our life at times of conflict and confusion.

When people first come to clairvoyants and mediums, it is often just for a psychic reading about their life, rather than for evidence from the spirit world.

Other mediums might work differently, but when a person arrives for a first reading with me, I ask them not to tell me anything about themselves. Having welcomed them at the door, I make them feel comfortable, then I generally say, 'I hope your reading goes well; it could be fantastic or not at all helpful. I never know until we get started! Please be honest with me and answer "yes", "no" or "I don't know".'

For a psychic reading it is not necessary for the medium to embrace the spirits at all. A good psychic simply works with their own intuition and gut instinct. They will be able to look at the person facing them and, by focusing their sensitivity on the sitter, tell that person what she or he has done in the past, what they are doing now, and also outline the person's current emotional state and general health.

When I am doing a reading, I often close my eyes, and sometimes I go so deep and the words and feelings come through so quickly, I don't even know what I am saying, and I remember very little afterwards. At other times I keep my eyes open and focus on a corner cabinet or some other inanimate object, so that I am not distracted by the client's body language. When I get to the end of the reading, I ask the person if they have any questions or wish to touch upon anything I have not brought up. Sometimes they then pluck up courage and ask me questions about relationships, work, finances, and I do my best to answer.

After readings, I am very touched when I receive lovely thank you letters saying things like: 'My mum and I came to see you for a one-to-one reading, and the experience was life-changing. Now I always keep in mind what you told me and I know this will help me and Mum for the rest of our lives.'

One of the hardest things any person is called upon to bear in this world is the death of a child, and no words can truly convey the sheer intensity of the pain, grief and devastation that a mother or father feels when confronted with the loss of a son or daughter.

'Explain to me why children and young people die,' is the most heartbreaking challenge that a medium comes across.

All I can offer is that we don't come from this world and we do not belong solely to it. Perhaps having achieved a particular purpose during any one lifetime, there is no need for us to hang around. In effect, we are saying to our loved ones, 'Right, darlings, I'm off now. I'm going back home to the spirit world.'

Life, I believe, is rather like an extended away-day, an assault course that can be horribly messy at times, but dying is like a cleansing shower accompanied by 'Welcome back'.

My spirit guides would answer: 'Our world is your true home, and time spent on earth is for you to learn what you need to learn in order to develop and for your spirit to grow. So, whether you are there on earth for a short or long stay, you will eventually return home.'

For me, life – whether short or long – is all about learning how to uncover more layers of who we are in order that we can progress spiritually, and I have known the most amazingly positive things to come from a parent losing a child. A mother will never fully get over her grief, but she may feel inspired to start a children's charity or a society to help other mothers come to terms with their grief. From deep suffering, then, good can come.

Any one of our lifetime's lessons might not be personal. It is said that there are children being born at this time who are coming to us from higher levels of the spirit. Reincarnated as light-bearers, they go out of their way to help others and to help us understand what life is really about. Like Gandhi, Martin Luther King, Mother Teresa and the Dalai Lama, they have the kind of sensitivity that shows others, by example, that life is not just about material things, it is about developing the spiritual self, creating light and harmony, and changing the world for the better.

Each life and death, though, has individual results, and we must never underestimate the grief of a mother or father who is just coming to terms with the fact that they can no longer give their much-loved child a hug in this lifetime. The realisation that you cannot put your arms around a memory can be totally heart-rending and overwhelming at times.

Without a shadow of doubt, I also believe that when a baby or child is taken into the spirit world, members of their families, such as grandparents or great-grandparents, or people who have had links to their family, take the child under their wing. I am certain that children are never allowed to be on their own, and that they are always enfolded by love. I also believe that when certain people in this world pass over, some of them elect to carry on with the work that they were doing when they were alive. I imagine, for example, that midwives, nurses, doctors and nannies are there waiting to heal, coax and nurture children before passing them over to family members in the spirit world.

About six years ago, when I was doing readings in my own home, a young couple in their early thirties arrived for their appointment. As they walked in, although it was a warm summer's evening, I sensed a chill and the presence of overwhelming grief hovering all around them. Having asked them to take a seat at my dining room table, I sat down opposite them and went through my usual procedure of asking them not to tell me anything. I then closed my eyes and began to read for them.

'You've recently lost a child?' I said, pausing for them to reply. Then, as there was no response, I added, 'Please say "yes" or "no".'

The man opposite me suddenly became very surly and aggressive. 'We're saying nothing,' he said. 'It's up to you to tell us.'

'Well,' I said, sensing how deeply he was hurting, 'I'm saying you *have* lost a child – and that all you have to do is say "yes" and we can continue.'

'Yes – we have lost a child,' the woman replied in a broken voice.

Her husband was not pleased and he gave her a look as if to say, 'Don't you *dare* say another word.'

'From this moment on,' I said, winging a frantic 'help me' prayer to the spirits, 'if I get anything wrong, I can only say it is me, the instrument, *not* the spirits. But I know that my spirit guide, Zintar, is with us now, and he is telling me that you lost your child six months ago.'

It was obvious from both their expressions that this was true.

'Thank you, Zintar,' I murmured silently. Then I closed my eyes and prayed fervently that the spirits would bring some evidence to this grieving couple that their child was well and happy in the spirit world. When I next opened my eyes, there, as clear as day, was a vision of a blonde, curly haired little girl standing by the door of my dining room. She was about three years of age and was dressed in a dark green velvet party dress.

As I finished describing the child I had seen in the doorway, I noticed that the husband's expression had not changed and that he was still looking at me with deep distrust written all over his face. The woman, however, ignoring what he had said earlier, started to sob.

'She was blonde,' she said, 'she did have curls and, yes, we buried her in her favourite green velvet party dress.'

Just as she finished speaking, I saw the same child standing in the doorway, but this time, just for a moment, she was emaciated and had no hair, and I knew that she had had leukaemia. As soon as I had registered this, as quick as a flash I saw her again as she was in the spirit world. Bright as a button, chirpy and cheeky, with her curly hair and her little green dress on, she was saying, 'I'm all better now.'

Having passed on this evidence, the man sat staring down at his hands, his face now hidden from me, and the woman continued crying into her handkerchief.

'I would love to pass on lots more information to you,' I said, turning to the mother, 'but I don't think I will be able to give you much more, because your daughter has not been passed over that long, and this communication isn't easy. I do know that she is here right now, though, and that she knows her room in your home is completely unchanged and that you often light a candle in there and lie on her bed.'

Without the husband needing to say anything, I realised that the actions I had just described were very common among mothers who have lost a child, and I wasn't surprised that he raised his head and was looking at me in a very suspicious way.

'I *wish*,' I said to him, 'that I could give you her name. She is saying something, but I just can't get it.'

He was not impressed. 'I *want* to know her name,' he said in a stony voice. 'Tell me her name.'

Closing my eyes again, I prayed once more to Zintar and the spirits, then listened to the inner voice that came through.

'I am now being told that you have another little girl,' I said to the father, 'and the spirits are telling me that this daughter is living.'

I did not open my eyes, but I heard his sharp intake of breath.

Having paused, I called on the spirits again. 'This man's need is *so* great,' I told them. 'Please help me to help him.'

The next moment I heard myself saying to the father: 'Your little girl in the spirit world is telling me that her sister's name is Sarah.' Then, without waiting for him to reply, I called out, 'All right, darling, I *can* hear you now. Your sister's name is Sarah and your name is . . .?'

I still could not catch what she was saying.

'Your sister's name is Sarah,' I repeated, 'and your name is . . .?'

Suddenly, as if in a big swirl, the name came to me.

'Louise?' I said aloud to the couple. 'Your daughter's name is Louise.'

On hearing that, the floodgates opened and the husband burst into tears. He had been so wary, so negative, yet he so desperately wanted and needed the connection.

That reading was a turning point for me, too. Until then I

had always been clairvoyant and known that I could get some things right in a reading, but on that occasion I felt that I had truly risen to meet a person's need and that, with the spirits' help, the reading had been perfect.

I had a similar experience one night when I was booked to go to a house in Hornchurch, Essex, to do a 'home visit' – a one-to-one reading for a group of six people. The first person who sat down for their readings was a well-built, muscular bloke, who had a shaved head and looked a real hard case. When I first set eyes on him and heard his gruff voice, I thought, 'Oh God!'

Sitting opposite me, his arms folded, he began by staring me out and, not surprisingly, the reading began very badly. I talked about his work, his house, his relationships, but it was all very mundane and rather hit-and-miss on the psychic level. His gruff responses were simple: 'yes', 'maybe', 'possibly'.

Almost imploring the spirit world, I said, '*Please*, come and let this man know something of your presence. If he has anyone in spirit, let me know if they are there, tell me their names. Anything.'

There was no response and, feeling totally defeated, I was about to give up and say, 'OK, you've won. Just go back to the others', when I was suddenly aware of something warm and heavy on my lap.

'There's something on my lap,' I said to the guy. 'I don't know what it is, but I know it is there and it feels heavy.'

'Is it the spirit of a dog?' I wondered. 'Or a cat?'

Suddenly I felt human arms wrap around my neck. 'What on earth is it?' I thought, mystified. 'It's far too big to be a baby.'

I then went into a semi-trance-like state and, having surrendered all sense of myself, I allowed the message to flow through me. Zintar came to me, as he always does when a child comes through, and I heard myself saying to the man opposite me, 'Your son is here in the spirit world and he wishes to bring his love to you and to thank you for always carrying him. He is also thanking you for bathing him and putting him to bed and, although he could not say the words in life, he wishes to say he loves you.'

I could hear the man starting to cry, but I was still in the trance-like state and, in a vision, I saw a severely handicapped child, aged about seven, who had the physical and mental attributes of a baby. In the spirit world, though, this child could speak without difficulty, was articulate and eloquent and, in my mind, I knew he was healed and very happy that he could run, jump and skip, and that he was saying to his father, 'Look! I can do all these things now.'

When I passed this on, it meant everything to the man.

That reading has lived with me ever since that night, because it was totally wonderful to see a child who was broken become so whole, and because the vision came to me just as I was about to give up.

The man, who was indeed a hard case, was not in the habit of displaying any kind of emotion, but he was totally dissolved by the experience. He had done his damnedest to resist and put me off my stride, but the power of the boy's spirit was so strong that he had succeeded in getting through against those odds.

A few years ago I was asked to do a demonstration in the lounge of a very large house in Crawley, Sussex, for about thirty people. It was a lovely autumnal evening and the people were so pleased to have me there that I felt I could not put a foot wrong.

One of my last readings concerned a handicapped boy who could not walk and who wanted to send a message to one of the young girls in the room to thank her for looking after him so lovingly when he was alive.

'What's your name?' I kept asking him, but all I could hear in reply was the word 'peanut'.

Having described the boy to the girl, who was obviously finding it very emotional to hear from him, I said, 'I don't know why, but he keeps on calling out "peanuts".'

'That's his name,' she gasped. 'We always called him "Peanut" because he had an unusually shaped head that looked like a peanut! We never told his parents we called him that, but we did. It was just an endearment.'

That evening, as I drove home, I was *so* elated. That occasion was yet another confirmation that we cannot die and that we do not forget those we love and those who love us when we are alive. Although by then I had been allowed to be the channel for such experiences on an almost daily basis, I had never become blasé or taken my psychic gift for granted. Far from it; I often thought – and still think – that I am more of a hindrance than a help to the spirit people. But there are days like that when everything comes together as it should, and there is such clarity of communication for the people concerned.

Recently, I was having a good day at the College of Psychic Studies, and among many things I described was a woman's husband. Having told her he was a stockily built, muscular man with dark hair who drove a lorry, I then astonished her by giving her the lorry's registration number! It really is amazing what the spirits will convey to us sometimes.

When the next fellow came in for a reading, however, I could not get a word – nothing. He was a very smart, handsome young man, and the first thing I said to him was, 'You're very apprehensive.'

'No, I'm not,' he replied curtly.

'You're very aggressive.'

'No, I'm not.'

'I'm sorry,' I said, 'but I am not the medium for you. Please go back to reception, get your money back and book a session with another medium on another day. I wish you the very best of luck.'

A few minutes later the receptionist phoned through to me and said, 'That's *very* strange. That man has been sent back to reception by four other clairvoyants, and each one has said they cannot get a reading for him. You were the fifth and final one. He has now been told that if you can't read for him, he shouldn't come again.'

It is always a pity when people, who seemingly want it so much, cannot receive, but I am always very honest with them. I send them home or suggest that they come back the following week when they might be in a more receptive state. On average, this happens with about one in ten people. Maybe they are just not ready to listen, maybe it just isn't their time. If they do come back and it still does not work, I then suggest that they should try another medium.

I was sorry for the young man, but his energy was totally incompatible with mine – and the other mediums' – and there was the lack of a good spirit person to help. Sometimes we just have to accept that spirits do not want – or are unable – to make contact, perhaps because they did not have a close relationship with the person who is asking for the reading.

Certainly, some people find it easier to receive spirits than others, and I personally find it much easier to receive the spirits when I am happy, alert and really up for it. Because we humans have physical bodies that tire, we vibrate at a slower rate than those in the spirit world. Spirits, however, are free from their bodies and from the hustle and bustle of worldly affairs, and their energy is lighter. When they wish to connect with us, they have to dip their vibration, slow their energy and concentrate on coming back to the density of the world. If the person they then communicate with is happy, the spirit finds it easier to make the connection, but if someone is very depressed, distraught or ailing, it is harder for the spirits to get through to them.

Usually, when a person's grief becomes easier to bear a year or so after the passing of their loved one, they will be more receptive.

When I am eventually able to give a message to a mother who has been desperately yearning to hear from a child, she might ask why she hasn't been able to reach him or her before. I then explain that it is all about energy levels – and her energy has been too low for a medium to be able to help her. Sometimes, too, the spirit has to be shown how to come through and blend with the mind of the medium.

The living person must also *want* the communication! On one memorable occasion, when I was on stage at a public demonstration, I said, 'I have a man here who tells me his name is Robert. Who knows Robert in the spirit world?'

No one.

'I've got a man here,' I repeated, 'whose name is Robert and he is telling me he wants to apologise to a lady here tonight for what he did to her when she was a child.'

Still no one put up their hand.

'This man . . .' I persisted.

Suddenly a woman put up her hand.

'Darling,' I said, crossing to the side of the stage, 'I was just about to give up on this spirit. Do you know Robert? And do you understand what he is trying to say?'

'Yes, I know him,' she murmured through gritted teeth, 'and I don't want to speak to him.'

Despite the gasp in the auditorium, there was nothing I could do at that moment. I did, however, make a point of speaking to her when I came off stage after the demonstration.

'He was my uncle,' she said, 'and although he pretended to love me, he sexually abused me when I was a child. He is the *last* person I want to speak to or see ever again, but having received your message tonight, I do at least feel a bit better knowing he is at last sorry for what he did.'

'Do you believe animals have souls?' is another question I am frequently asked, and my answer is, 'Yes, I am absolutely sure that what happens to children when they pass also happens to our pets.' Animals, whether they are domestic, farm or wild animals, do have souls, and it is also possible that they have had other incarnations. For example, I think domestic animals – dogs, cats and horses – who have been at the receiving end of human love and companionship develop very human qualities and have the potential to progress over a period of time from an animal to a human embodiment.

I also know that pets can fulfil an important purpose in our life: they can draw things out of us and help to develop our emotional life and our ability to give and receive love.

One example of an animal wishing to communicate with its master occurred when I was working at the College of Psychic Studies. On this occasion, when I was doing a reading for a rather shy middle-aged man, the spirit of his mother came through.

'My son's always been very much a loner,' she said, 'and he has always loved spending his time out of doors.'

Having readily accepted the evidence in this message, the man said, 'It's true. I've always enjoyed my own company and I love walking alone through the countryside.'

Just as I was getting to the end of his reading and about to let him go, I was startled by a vision that contained a huge dark shape.

'Oh my God!' I exclaimed, as I looked again in my mind's eye. 'There's a *huge* horse standing right behind you.'

'What does it look like?' he asked, his face instantly lighting up.

'It's a big chestnut, with a somewhat crooked V-shaped white blaze across its nose and a white star on the centre of his chest.'

As I was describing the horse, I could sense it planting thoughts in my head.

'He's just loving you *so* much,' I said, as I repeated the horse's thoughts out loud, 'and he's thanking you for being his friend and for letting him go.'

At that moment the man's shoulders crumpled and he broke down and cried.

'He was my best friend,' he said softly when he was sufficiently recovered to speak, 'and although I didn't want to let him go, I had to call the vet for his sake. He was so ill and suffering so much, he had to be put to sleep.'

I totally sympathised with the man's grief. When my Yorkshire Terrier, Madonna, died of old age while I was out of the country, I was totally devastated. For me, it was a very emotional event. After hearing on the Wednesday that Madonna was ill and that a friend had taken her to the vet, I later got a call from the vet informing me that nothing could be done to save her.

'It would be kinder,' he said, 'for you to give your permission for me to release her from the pain and put her to sleep.'

I was choked, but I knew I had to agree for Madonna's sake. Afterwards I could not stop crying. She was such a character, such a little madam, such an important part of me that I couldn't envisage life without her. Emotionally drained by the experience, I fell into a deep sleep. A couple of hours later, I found myself waking up to a vision of a lady who had loved Madonna in life and who was now cradling her in her arms. In this vision, Madonna was no longer old. She was young and sprightly, wagging her tail, and her eyes were bright with no sign of the cloudiness that had come with old age. It was a totally wonderful scene that left me feeling so comforted that, some weeks later, I found myself breaking a vow that I had made on the day of her death.

'I will *never* have another dog,' I had sobbed that day. 'Losing them is just *too* painful and I can't go through that again.'

Thanks to the vision, though, I was soon able to set this vow aside and I found myself driving up to Hull to pick up an eight-week-old Border Terrier puppy that I called Archie. This little character will never replace Madonna in my affections, but I know that he will become as big a part of my life as she did.

The lady holding Madonna in the vision was Stuart's mother. That was very comforting because, when his mother was alive, Stuart had taken Madonna with him on many of his visits to her and his mum had really bonded with her. I knew that she would take good care of her.

I had never met Stuart's mother myself, but I recognised her at once in the vision. She was a very glamorous lady, and some years earlier, when she was still alive, I had had another vision of her. On this occasion I had found myself sitting next to her in a softly lit room that was decorated with a pretty floral wallpaper.

'Tony,' she had said, looking at me as if she knew me really well and trusted me, 'I have cancer and I haven't long to live. Please don't worry Stuart by telling him what I have just told you, but *please* promise me that you will keep an eye on him.'

When the vision faded and I woke up in my own home, my first thought was: '*Oh God*! Stuart's mum is going to die'. My second thought was: 'I will do everything I can to comfort him when the time comes.'

Within four months, his mother had passed. Stuart was only twenty-two and I just couldn't begin to imagine how difficult his mother's death was for him. If I had lost my mum at that age I would have been totally grief-stricken. I made a vow that I would do what his mother had asked me to do and always keep an eye on him and make sure that he was OK.

It was a year or so before I told Stuart about my out-of-body experience with his mum, and when I did he was comforted to know that she had known that she was dying and had had time to prepare herself for the event.

One day, many years later, I heard a lady spirit singing, 'Happy birthday to you . . . Happy birthday to you . . .', and I knew it was Stuart's mum.

'Stuart,' I asked him later, 'is today someone's birthday in your family?'

'No,' he said, looking at the date on his watch.

'It *has* to be,' I replied. 'I've just heard your mum singing "Happy birthday".'

'Well it isn't,' he replied.

'That's very strange,' I thought.

Then suddenly Stuart said, 'What *is* today's date?'

When I told him, he realised the date on his watch was not correct and that it was actually his younger brother's birthday on that very day!

When members of my own family come through, they do not often come for a particular reason, but they do tend to come at times like Christmas, and they also remind me about family birthdays! I talk to my dead relatives every day. I don't go on for ages, but I am always mindful of their quiet presence and I speak to them in the same way that we talk to our living relatives or friends.

When people are open and receptive, they are always surprised by how often their dead loved ones wish to communicate with them. I often feel the presence of my grandmas and granddads, and my Aunt Grace.

One of my last meetings with Aunt Grace on earth was memorable. She wasn't very well after returning from a holiday in Turkey, and we all thought she might have a tummy bug. She seemed to be getting better, but she wasn't eating very much. She was seventy-six at this time, and I used to go round to her bungalow to go through her bills, sort out any queries, and do everything I could for her.

One day, as I was leaving, I gave her my usual kiss on the cheek and said, 'Bye, Grace, I'll give you a call later in the week and let you know when I'll be round to see you again.'

Unusually, I also put my arms around her and gave her a hug. As she held on to me, she said, 'D'you know, Tony, I *really* love you. You do know that, don't you.'

Now that was something we never said. We knew that we loved one another, and that we had always been mates, but we never expressed our love in words.

'I really love you, too,' I said. 'Don't worry about anything, Grace, I'll always come and see you.'

She then gave me a strange, penetrating look, which stopped me in my tracks and unnerved me as I shut the front gate behind me. The usual routine was that I would then wave all the way to the end of the street, but on this occasion, as I did this, I felt the presence of my nan and granddad and heard a whole host of voices from the spirit world singing the Vera Lynn song, 'We'll meet again, don't know where, don't know when, But I know we'll meet again some sunny day . . .'

It was as if they were letting me know gently and saying,

'She's going, you know, but you will meet again, some sunny day.'

The voices were so clear, so overwhelming, I could not bear to look back at Grace. I just kept on walking and waving, and when I got into my car I broke down. Soon after that we learned that Aunt Grace was not suffering from a tummy bug, she had stomach cancer.

I went to see her often during the last three weeks of her life. On the day she died, we had a call from the hospital to get there as soon as we could, but when we arrived she had already gone and had been laid out. Although she looked peaceful, it was very hard to leave her there.

When we left the hospital, I went back with my parents to their house, and as I took the key from Mum to open the door, I was the first person to enter. When I opened the door to the lounge, I was in for a very pleasant shock. There, only an hour or so after she had died, was Aunt Grace, standing by the television in the corner of the room.

'You know I'm all right,' I heard her saying in a smiley voice, 'but keep telling your mum I'm OK.'

She has come back to me many times since then.

After Aunt Grace died, I telephoned my friend Sharon Harvey, who's a very good medium, currently living in Lincoln. She knew my aunt Grace had been very ill and, when she learned of her death, she told me she was going to a psychic meeting that evening and would mention to the group that my aunt had died. She would not, she added, tell them her name.

When she phoned me the next day, she said that there had been a young boy called Jonathan in the group, and that after he had begun to meditate, he had said, 'There's a woman here whose name is Grace. She always smoked, liked her gin and tonic, and was a real trouper and party lady.'

It was a fantastic spirit message that gave me all the necessary evidence that Grace had made it into the spirit world and was already returning just three days after her death.

I also received a message from Grace when I was sitting with Janet Parker, another medium.

'I've got two ladies here,' she said. 'They are sisters, like two peas in a pod, very glamorous, very East London women, who are telling me they came from Walthamstow.'

I was so astonished because you cannot get better than that. Aunt Grace and her sister, Kath, who was my nan, loved each other and were inseparable in life. There were six girls in that family and a boy, Eric, who died. They had lived in Walthamstow and they were East End princesses.

When Kath was six years old, her mother, who was only just forty, died. Her father, William, was a bit of a drunk who hardly gave a thought to her and the other kids who had been left in his care. They lived above a shop in a two-storey flat in Wood Street, Walthamstow, and when they all started to get on his nerves, he decided he had had enough, couldn't cope any longer, and that he would put the children in an orphanage.

On the evening before he planned to do this, he returned from the pub, drunk as usual, and started climbing the rickety stairs to his bedroom. To his horror, just as he reached the top step, he saw a white glow, then the spirit of his dead wife standing before him.

'If you put my kids into a home,' she said, raising a menacing fist, 'I will haunt you till the day you die.'

He was so terrified, he decided to ask his dead wife's mother – the kids' old granny – to move in with them, and he never again considered putting the children into an orphanage!

There are a lot of people who debunk the existence of spirits and of mediums and mediumship, saying that any belief in such matters is only for the ignorant, for people who are desperate. But the story of my nan, Kath, and her father, William, is but one example of a man whose mind and beliefs were changed by one powerful encounter with a spirit. It was a pretty good experience for the children, too – one that altered the course of their life and allowed them to grow up in a family, cared for by a loving granny, rather than an orphanage.

I never feel panicked by not knowing all the answers and not being able to help or satisfy everybody who comes to me for a reading. I realise that what I achieve is just the tip of the iceberg, and that any insight I have is entirely dependent on my own spiritual evolution. When I am more spiritually advanced, I will be blessed with deeper insight and I will be able to help more people.

Meanwhile, I am happy to do my best and am more than happy for everyone to have their own beliefs. Life, with its variety of cultures, ideas, thoughts, beliefs and different ways of doing things, is wonderful. The only thing that upsets me is religious fanaticism – sects or groups who think they are the only ones who have all the answers and who try to imprint these on everyone else's way of thinking.

I believe we are meant to be different, and that each of us has to learn to think and sort things out for ourselves. If a person says, 'I don't believe in anything other than the fact that I am flesh and blood, and here, and that I am food for the worms after that', then that is their right. If that is what they think, then that is where they are at right now, and no one should bully or browbeat them into thinking otherwise.

I certainly believe that I have been born into this world for a reason, and that part of that reason is to live out this lifetime working as a medium, telling people what I see, hear and feel. And if just one person who has read this book is sufficiently intrigued to go on and investigate the paranormal further, I will be a *very* happy man!

My ideal place to meditate and to open my mind to the spirit world is a sun-dappled wood or forest. These places can be as awe-inspiring and as uplifting as a church with stained glass windows, especially if the forest has a canopy of leaves with little shafts of light coming through them.

One of my greatest joys in life is looking up at the sky. Sometimes it looks just as if the Great Spirit has painted the most amazing canvas, using orange, red and purple colours. At other times, towards the end of a cloudy day and just after it has rained, the sun manages a final breakthrough and the resulting shaft of light looks just like a rainbow-coloured staircase leading from heaven to earth.

When I was a child I told my mum that angels came down that staircase to take all the people who had died, and who were now waiting at the bottom of it, up to heaven. As ever, my mum, who always let me express myself without making harsh judgements, was very good about this.

'Oh,' she replied, 'that's a *lovely* thing to say, Tony.'

I do not know who raised my eyes to the sky and planted that seed in my young head, but I am so glad they did. It created something that grew and brought me, along with other experiences, to where I am now.

6

'God Works in Mysterious Ways . . .'

When I am teaching at the college, on a good day I can feel the emotional temperature of the people in the room. Recently, I found myself sensing one woman, who had been to about four of the meetings, as a great black cloud. The energy she was emanating was so strong, it was affecting the atmosphere of the whole room – so much so that after about twenty minutes I decided to change tack from making clairvoyant links to self-healing. At least this succeeded in shifting the energy from negative to positive.

At the end of the class, the woman was the first person to spring up and try to leave, but I called her back.

'Alice, could you hold on a mo,' I said, 'I'd like to have a word with you.'

She looked very hesitant but nevertheless waited until the last person had left.

'I know something's wrong,' I said, gently. 'What's the matter?'

She immediately burst into tears.

Minutes later, she poured out her heart and told me that her husband, who had recently started drinking heavily, had beaten her up during the week. He knew she had found something wonderful in studying the paranormal and he was feeling threatened by this.

Meeting this kind of reaction in others is, to a greater or lesser degree, quite common when sensitives first begin work on a spiritual level. Fearing change in their partners or friends can cause some people to react very negatively and to come down on them like a ton of bricks. Likewise, some sensitives go through life wearing their hearts on their sleeve and, while they often make the best psychics and mediums, they can also be taken advantage of by other people.

What alerted me to Alice's state of mind that day is what we call an 'aura' – the energy that emanates from the spirit within the body. Everything in creation, even a leaf and a tree, has an auric field, and psychics, mediums and healers are aware of these auras pouring from a person's head or body. There is nothing new or space age about this! Since ancient times, artists have portrayed this effect in their works: ancient Indian sculptures, aboriginal rock paintings and American Indian totem poles all portray figures surrounded by areas of light that emanate from their bodies, and the halo in Christian religious art represents the golden glow of an aura around the head. The visible aura is an oval shape that can extend from just a few inches to several feet around the body, and at the head.

Auras are composed of different coloured rays, and the shape, colour and strength of these rays reflect our unique individual make-up and reveal our physical, emotional and spiritual state. *Red* is the colour of life and represents physical vigour, strength, energy and passion. *Orange* is associated with energy and health and indicates a strong personality. *Yellow* is associated with intellect and an optimistic nature, and golden-yellow is a sign of spiritual development. *Green* is the colour of nature, regeneration and healing, and shows a lively adaptable personality and a versatile mind. *Blue* is associated with idealism, integrity and inspiration. *Indigo* indicates a person who acts on their intuition and who rises above the physical world in their search for spiritual truth. *Violet* is the colour of spiritual enlightenment, insight and love. *Black and grey* reveal an aura that has been damaged by negative thoughts, emotions or illness. *White* represents ideals, truth and perfection.

Some psychics say that auras contain many layers that represent the different colours and energies, but I do not see them as layers. I see them as black and white or as a specific colour. I certainly notice that when I am with a person whose prime interest is in spiritual matters, I see high-frequency colours such as lilac, indigo, pale blue or silver. Likewise, when I am with someone who is extrovert, out-going or athletic, I see vibrant colours such as red and orange. If I see a crescent shape across the head, it indicates to me that the person is suffering from depression or grief. I recently saw black hovering in the area of a woman's breast and asked her if she had recently had a breast scan – was not surprised she then said she had been diagnosed with cancer and was about to go into hospital for an operation. I used to resist mentioning such things, but now that I am more confident I approach this in a sensitive way that never creates panic. In fact, it often has the reverse effect. The person finds it reassuring that I am able to sense that all is not well with them and they are grateful for the opportunity to talk to somebody. Sometimes, too, when there is a real trauma present in the person's body, I feel as if I am being kicked in the stomach.

Recently, when my first client of the day arrived, I could sense from her aura that she was in a nervous, jittery state, but when I looked beyond this I realised that it was only a surface thing. She was actually a beautiful, soulful person who was currently having a lot of problems with her eyesight. When her mother, who had recently died, came through it was a really lovely connection.

'Don't worry,' her mother wanted me to tell her. 'Your eyes

will never be so bad that you cannot continue to work as a fashion designer.'

The girl was absolutely thrilled. 'My greatest fear,' she told me, 'was that I would lose my ability to design and make clothes.'

The people who come to see me are from every income level and walk of life, and they do not belong to any particular religion or age group. Some of the young people – from eighteen upwards – come because they are looking for their pathway through life. They may feel different from others and sometimes they even have some indication that they have been reborn from a higher sphere and that they want to do something positive with their current life, such as becoming a doctor, healer or peace-keeper. Others come along hoping to resolve family issues and problems. Many come with unfinished business from their childhood and talk about horrendous experiences; others come with an open, enquiring mind and no particular agenda.

About eighty per cent of people who know me as a medium come because they want to speak to members of their family who have passed over. When I first started work as a medium, most of the people who came to see me were women aged between forty and sixty, but now a lot of younger people come for readings, and many of these, including the men, also come to my workshops and development seminars. When I am given free rein while doing a class, I always make an effort to create the right ambience. Candles and incense can transform a nondescript, poky little room into a sanctuary. I like to create the kind of atmosphere where people can walk out of the mayhem of their everyday life into a new environment.

For newcomers, the seminar may be the first step they have taken in relation to the paranormal and, although they may arrive in a very sceptical frame of mind, they often walk away a changed person because they have seen with their own eyes and heard with their own ears!

At one particular seminar in Scarborough, there was a guy called Chris. As soon as I set eyes on him I knew that he was a total cynic and that he would be very hard work, but I still took him into my group.

At the end of the weekend's final class, he confessed that he had only come along because he didn't believe a word of it and he had wanted to see how we faked it. By now, though, he had completely opened up and was clinging to me and crying.

'The seminar,' he said, 'has completely changed my life. I so *wanted* to believe it was all a trick, but you can't deny what you've seen and heard. I couldn't pretend to understand yet, but I know it isn't fake.'

On that occasion, among many other things, I had demonstrated trance mediumship. For some people this is the most evidential form of contact that is given to us by the spirit world because sometimes the spirits allow their voices to be heard, or they transplant their faces over the medium's face. It really is a very physical event in which I could be sitting with twenty-eight sceptics, but they would all see the same thing at the same time – another face could manifest over my own, for example. This is called transfiguration.

At a seminar in Eastbourne, attended by about seventy people, I held a séance. That evening my spirit guides, Zintar and Star, came through and spoke through me while I was in a trance. They also enabled some spirit people to enter my body and show themselves physically. It was a really successful evening because a girl I know quite well was present and her father came through. Afterwards she told me that it had been a very emotional experience because my face completely changed and she could see her dad's features, including his bushy eyebrows, transfigured on my face. They were then able to look at each other before he disappeared again.

Transfiguration is a very powerful form of mediumship, but I am only at an early stage of developing this skill. I hope to be a fully developed transfiguration medium one day, though.

A wonderful aspect of this kind of work is that sometimes when I play a tape back, I can hear the people present gasping because they are witnessing a spirit's face manifesting over my own. They may be mediums and psychics themselves, but even an ordinary non-psychic person would have been able to see what they saw.

Many years ago I was at a séance with Stuart and a group of other people, which was led by Colin Fry, a good friend of mine, who is a very powerful physical medium and a clairvoyant. During the course of that séance, as Colin went into a trance, we heard voices floating about in mid-air and spirits brushed past us and touched our hands. It was a hot day, but the temperature of the room suddenly dropped to freezing and, as Stuart bent down to pick up his water, he found it had frozen to the bottom of the glass. It was a totally amazing, mind-blowing experience.

'What are spirits trying to prove on such occasions?' is a commonly asked question. The answer is simply that they *can* do it! The spirits are there, just beyond the fringes of this world, and they want to make their presence felt in any way they possibly can. They are rather like children at times, constantly thinking up new ways to get our attention.

I have witnessed the phenomena of a table moving on its own volition on many occasions, and I can testify that there were no tricks involved. Without touching the table myself, I simply asked the people present to rest their fingers on it and then I called out loud and asked the spirits to move it. When all of a sudden the table moved, people's faces registered total shock and amazement.

The following event happened in my evening group at the college in the summer of 2003. The previous week, Alan, one of the members, had asked me if we could do some table-moving phenomena, and I had said, 'Yes – of course.' Alan, a lawyer aged about thirty-six, is the son and grandson of practising mediums, but, although he has always had a keen interest in the paranormal, he has only just started developing his own mediumship.

In the corner of the room that we use for our meetings, there is a very large, old table, which measures about six feet by four feet, and Alan asked if we could practise the table-moving phenomena on this. So the nine of us present heaved the table into the centre of the room, and when everybody had collected themselves I asked them to rest the tips of their fingers lightly on the table top, using the same kind of pressure they would apply if they were dusting talcum powder on to a baby's bum. Then I began to call on the spirits.

'Come on, darlings,' I urged. 'If you are there, shift the table for us, just to let us know that you are around.'

Within a minute or two, the table shifted, then continued to move around. This was by no means the first time we had witnessed this in the group, so the students were quite used to it. But this occasion was different. The incredibly heavy table, with just one finger on it, was actually moving along the wooden floor from one end of the room to the other. Up and down it went and we were all laughing because we felt that the spirits were having fun, too.

'Alan,' I said, joining in the spirits' playful mood, 'I've got a great idea. Get on the table.'

Now Alan weighs between eleven and twelve stone, but,

having done what I asked, he sat there cross-legged. Within a moment or two, the table, with him sitting on top of it, began whizzing up and down the room even faster than it had done before. When he eventually climbed off, I asked the spirits what else the table could do. After a moment we heard a gentle thud, followed by a rhythmic, repetitive knocking from beneath the table. As all fingertips were on top of the table and the knocking was coming from beneath it, there was no way that any of those present could have been responsible for the phenomena. It was wonderful! We all thoroughly enjoyed ourselves because it was a good, friendly energy, as if the spirits were celebrating and saying, 'We're here in the room with you. What else would you like us to do?'

Recalling this has reminded me that about five years ago, when my mum was talking to me about my nan, Kath, who had passed over in 1986, my dad was fooling around making spooky sound-effects.

'Once you're dead,' he then pronounced, 'you're dead, that's it – curtains! But if you're listening, Kath, my love, just do something to show me you're there.'

This was one tease he lived to regret!

That night he went to bed ahead of my mother, and the next thing Mum heard was his frantic voice calling her to come to the bedroom. When she went into the room, there was Dad, ashen faced, sitting up in the bed looking petrified. It took a few moments for him to make sense, but, when he did manage to speak coherently, he said that when he had first got into the bed and lain down, the bottom of the bed had moved as if someone had just sat on the end of it.

Now, my dad is not a fanciful man, and certainly not one to make things up, but, when he tried to ignore this event, it happened again, and this time the end of the bed started rocking up and down as if someone was repeatedly getting up then sitting down again.

'Oh God,' Dad cried out, remembering his earlier sarcastic challenge, 'if that's you, Kath, *please* stop it. *Please* don't do that!'

The movements continued for a while longer, and even became quite violent, which is when my dad called my mum upstairs.

Much later Mum told me that ever since Dad had had this experience, he had never said anything negative about spirits again.

'It gave him much food for thought!' she said.

The table-tilting incident also brings back memories of a holiday to Cairo. While there, I visited the Great Pyramid, its two massive neighbours and the Great Sphinx.

There on the plateau at Giza, my guide book informed me, Khufu, the grand king of the fourth Dynasty, had built the largest pyramid ever raised, and around it he had buried members of the royal family and his nobles. His two sons had then followed his lead and, by the end of the era, which became known as the 'age of the great pyramids', they had built their own pyramids, which were only slightly less grand than their father's. The second of the sons, Khafre, also fashioned the Great Sphinx, which sits in the old quarry on the western side of the pyramids' area.

My first glimpse of the mortuary complex was absolutely breathtaking and, like so many tourists before me, I was filled with awe and wonder.

Only one or two of the pyramids are open to the public each day, and on the day of my visit the site was packed with people from all over the world. It was like a meeting of the United Nations! Yet although there were so many tourists milling around, blinking in the sunshine and sagging in the heat, I was fortunate enough to find myself alone inside the Grand Gallery of the Great Pyramid, with only a sleepy guard who was not taking any notice of me. Standing very still, I took in my surroundings, hardly able to believe that I was in a place where ancient Egyptians had trod so many centuries ago.

Inside the Great Pyramid is a complex which contains three chambers – the king's chamber, the queen's chamber and the Grand Gallery – but only the huge Grand Gallery is open to the public. As I stood there I noted that on each of the granite-block walls were notices that read DO NOT TOUCH. But my fingers were *aching* to do precisely that. I was suffering from an irresistible urge to connect with the energy that I sensed those blocks contained. Finally, unable to resist, I threw a glance at the guard who was still looking the other way and reached out and placed the palms of my hands flat against the wall.

At the very instant my hands touched the wall, I felt this great surge of white light and energy cascade through my body. It was as if I had plugged myself into a major power source – a source so vibrant, so great that it was the life-force for every ray, every tiny speck of light that lit up, irradiated the universe.

Standing there, I felt as if I had become a human beacon and that my whole being was radiating outwards, empowered by the energy that was flowing through me. My whole body was alight, affected by an energy that seemed to be arising from within the granite blocks and travelling through my body to reach the sun, moon and stars before coming back to rest again.

I could have stood there forever, but the guard, completely oblivious of what I was experiencing, suddenly crossed over to me. Indicating the DO NOT TOUCH notices, he wagged a finger at me and moved me on.

Back in the outside world, I was aware that the brilliant light cast by the Egyptian sun was as nothing compared with the light and the energy that had been generated within the granite blocks of the Great Gallery. That light source had been so great, it had taken my breath away. For weeks afterwards, I was lit up, on cloud nine. I felt renewed, energised, healed of all weariness.

'Could this be what people called "pyramid power"?', I found myself wondering later.

I learned that many visitors before me had reported experiencing warm, top-to-toe tingling sensations when inside a pyramid, and that others had mentioned that they'd found themselves sleeping more soundly and experiencing much improved well-being after their visit. Some American scientists had also suggested that the actual shape of the pyramids – four-sided buildings with triangular sides – created a heightened energy field that altered the rate of physical, chemical and biological processes. I am certainly no scientist and, at the time of my visit, I didn't know any of this. But even when I did, I just *knew* that what I had experienced was a tremendous spiritual charge. It was as if the finger of God had touched me.

One interesting aside from my visit to the pyramids at Giza is that, having found myself awe-struck and wondering how they had been built, my mind connected with the table-tilting phenomenon.

The actual methods that were used to construct the pyramids have puzzled investigators throughout the ages, and one recent theory has suggested that a sloping ramp was wound around the pyramid that was being raised and then left in position as the pyramid grew upwards. When the core was complete, the ancient Egyptians then positioned the capstone, which brought the pyramid's height to 135 metres, and added the rest of the sheathing – a fine-quality limestone – possibly from the top down. As each level was finished, the ramp was dismantled.

Now for another theory!

When I was preoccupied with these thoughts, my spirit guides reminded me that when we use our collective spiritual energy to connect with a heavy inanimate object, the object can become as light as a feather and can be tilted or moved. I also believe that the pyramids were constructed at a time when there were very special people – mystics and seers – who knew how to draw on the same eternal energy. Having placed their hands and fingertips on the massive slabs, they could have used their collective energy in the same way that we, with the help of spirits, use ours to tilt or move tables.

I love the idea of those awesome pyramids being constructed in this way. I know the eternal energy is available for us to 'plug' into, and I certainly had a very real sense of this when I touched the walls of that pyramid.

People often ask me about séances, which is a rather outdated term now. The word séance simply means a meeting at which people attempt to receive messages from the spirits of the dead. Historically, a séance would be held in a darkened room, invariably lit by a red light. Even modern-day mediums use subdued lighting and favour a red light.

'Why do we use red lights?' I once asked an elderly medium.

'Years ago when we only had candles and no electric lights,' he replied, 'we often worked in rooms where there was a coal fire alight that created a reddish-orange glow in the room, and that red glow became something that was used by mediums when they wanted to create subdued lighting and a certain atmosphere. So now, when we use our red lamps at séances, it recreates that wonderful atmosphere that's created by a fire.'

These days, some mediums use green or blue lights to create different energies in the room, but I am a traditionalist and always use red.

When I am conducting a séance, I close my eyes, drop into a trance and wait for my spirit guide to speak through me, then directly to the person or persons who are with me. In a séance environment, what can happen is that Zintar may come through and say to the people attending, 'A little less light,' and once the lights have been switched off and we have sat for a short time in a pitch-black room, he says, 'We're ready now.' The red light is then switched on and he says, 'We are going to start showing ourselves now,' and, to varying degrees of clarity, the red light reveals the spirits' faces implanted over my face.

In the past there were some very famous physical mediums who conducted séances. Mrs Gunning, the fruit-and-flowers medium, was just one. But there were also others who could, for example, demonstrate what is known as the independent direct voice. In this, the spirits do not speak through the medium's vocal chords, they speak from anywhere in the room. One moment the disembodied voice is to the left of you, the next moment it's to the right – and sometimes there is more than one voice. This is a very rare phenomena that requires a unique form of mediumship, but I have witnessed it on a couple of occasions.

Certain things can have a detrimental effect on the quality of a medium's mediumship. The one that has the greatest adverse effect on me is heat. Summer is difficult for me because the rooms I find myself in are often too hot. Likewise, if I am tired I cannot work. My best evenings have always been on crisp, clear, cold winter nights when there is not a cloud in the sky.

I also feel very sad when I arrive at a venue only to find that I am preaching to the converted, who have become very blasé, and there is no excitement or sense of anticipation in the room.

On one really disastrous occasion about ten years ago, I found myself in a Spiritualist church close to where I live in Essex. Having got up on the platform, I discovered I was spiritually deaf, dumb and blind! I could not sense a single spirit or receive a single message. There was nothing I could do. It was a zero event.

'Thank you for coming, ladies and gentlemen,' I had to announce, 'but I am very sorry to say I have nothing for you. Would you like to ask me some spiritual questions instead . . .?'

It could have been that the spirits were testing me, but, as I had previously done a couple of good demonstrations and was feeling very confident, I think it was a test for people who had become too blasé.

If, by way of contrast, I go to an unlikely venue, such as a function room at the back of a pub, I often find that the people are buzzing with excitement and are really looking forward to the event. The energy that emanates on these occasions is brilliant. I *love* that and I feel I have a real job of work to do on behalf of the spirits!

I must also add, though, that because mediums suffer heartaches, pain and grief like everyone else, our vibrations can sometimes become very low, rather like a battery running down. In the spirit world, however, the energy is clear and vibrates at a faster rate. As a medium, you have to learn to adjust your vibration. Some of us can do this quite naturally, others have to train themselves so that they can tune in more easily to the spirits. As mediums we are always in the middle of the two worlds and it is up to us to get our audience to raise their energies so that the spirit people, who are able to lower their energies, can marry up with us midway between heaven and earth. This is where good mediums operate. If we cannot get that balance right, then the work can be very difficult.

If I am on stage, working at a new venue, I am a little more apprehensive than usual. Mediums do not have the benefit of rehearsals or the help of a warm-up guy to get the crowd focused and in the right mood, and we do not have scripts. I cannot think of any other occasion when Joe Public pays money to watch somebody perform who has done nothing to prepare for the audience. There is nothing a medium can do, other than be a medium!

I do not experience the same degree of stage fright that other performers, such as singers and actors, have to contend with. This is because, at one level, the performance I am about to do has little to do with me. All I can hope is that I will be a good channel, who is able to do the spirit world justice – and who will enable the people present to receive something life-enhancing.

Just before stepping on to a stage, I usually reassure myself by saying, 'Whatever happens, happens. It has nothing to do with me. I just hope that the people who have turned up are going to be receptive and open to the spirit people.'

As soon as I am on stage, all these thoughts drop away, which is probably just as well otherwise my own mind and other distractions would get in the way. At times, when everything falls into place, an hour can feel like ten minutes because I am so filled with energy and exhilaration.

At a personal level, because I genuinely feel I have nothing to prove, I think to myself: 'I am going to tell you exactly what enters my mind and if it proves to be a great connection, that's great. If it's terrible, I will apologise.'

Sometimes the links are fuzzy and I struggle! This can be because I am stressed, or I have not had enough sleep, or the atmosphere of the venue is totally out of sync. All negative factors can affect me. Clairvoyance requires a very subtle blend of energy. When the energies are up-beat and high, rather like the energy generated by a party, you cannot put a foot wrong.

'Why do we get illnesses and diseases?' is another question that I meet frequently in my work, and I have always been consistent in the way I answer it. The clue lies in the meaning of the word 'disease'. Disease – dis-ease – means ill at ease. By saying this, though, the last thing I want to imply is that every negative thought or stress we experience will lead to disease. Too many of these, however, can certainly set up a ripple, which can become a wave, then a tidal wave that can over-whelm us if we do not see the error of our ways and take action. Balance and measure in our lives is everything, and I sincerely believe that a person who is born healthy only becomes dis-eased and ill when they get into the habit of disregarding or mistreating their body.

When we accept that we have a divine as well as a physical self – and we do not constantly subject ourselves to extremes – we live in harmony with our spiritual self, are more centred, more balanced and measured, and therefore healthier. In this state of mind we are more positive and prepared to open ourselves up to the Great Spirit's universal power and energy, through practices such as meditation, and we do not create negative stresses which deplete our energy and allow illness to take over our body. As an individual, I am only too happy to testify that although I do not always recognise or acknowledge the blessings I receive, I am aware that I am helped and guided by the creative force behind our universe. If I did not have this belief, I know I would be out of sync and physically, emotionally and mentally unbalanced, and that I would not be topped up, so to speak, by that universal energy. When we are out of balance, we leave ourselves open to disease and illness.

In my work I see a lot of stressed-out people whose bodies have become totally out of sync because their lives are unmeasured – too much hassle and too much rushing around accompanied by too little nourishment and too little or too much sleep – and they have not taken sufficient steps to stop and take stock and renew their energies. In this situation, things can become very stagnated and, over a period of time, can create dis-ease.

I know people are often criticised for suggesting that we bring our health and disability troubles upon ourselves, but this may not be far from the truth. The law of karma is a natural law, and I believe that we are responsible for our own destiny and that how we choose to live this life affects the next. I do not see this as any kind of God-inflicted punishment, recompense or retribution, however. It really is simply Natural Law – cause and effect – and whatever the result of any one lifetime or situation, there is always a purpose and something positive that we can learn through being challenged.

It has been suggested that when we are born, we choose the right body for that lifetime's mission. It could simply be that we realise that our soul – our spirit – can overcome any challenge and will learn to be positive in the face of adversity. The words we repeat in our head, 'I can't slow down', 'I can't live any differently', or, on the positive side, 'I can change', and 'I will survive' are indeed sentences – life-and-death sentences!

The questions 'Why me?', 'Why am I suffering like this?', are natural and understandable. But they stem from the misguided – and damaging – idea that God, the Great Spirit, is a puppet master who enjoys pulling our strings and making this or that happen! That is *not* how it is. I believe we are given free will and that we ourselves make all life's choices. For example, by the time I am sixty, I could be living in Miami running a spiritual retreat, but I could also, if I decided to take that course, be reaping the seeds of a lifetime of constant partying and be living as an alcoholic in an East London bedsit. Either way, it would be *my* decision, not God's! If I listen, if I am true to myself rather than just following every whim, then I will be exactly where I need to be.

I fervently believe that we begin life with free will, but also with a blueprint – a map for this life. I also believe that each of us has a guardian angel, a spirit guide, whose purpose is to help us in every way they can to complete this particular journey. Our part in this is to listen to that 'still, small voice of calm' within us, and to be prepared to be 'reclothed', when-ever necessary, 'in our rightful mind'. If, however, we remain hell-bent on self-destruction, then we are not going to achieve what we need to achieve in any one lifetime.

Sometimes when people who are experiencing challenges in their lives come to see me, I offer them the following thought: 'Why not begin to enjoy life and even embrace the difficulties and obstacles in your way!' Then, while they are looking at me as if I have taken leave of my senses, I add: 'Let it be. Let the negativity flow and get to grips with it. *Why*? Because you can learn so much from it. What we cannot do is run away from a problem because that same problem will keep re-presenting itself until we face up to it.'

I do not say this to everyone, but this approach can work! Sometimes a person just needs a jolt, a chance to see a problem from a different perspective. He or she needs to believe that, with the right attitude, things can get better and, within a matter of months, their attitude to life can change and they can become stronger and more positive. The crap in our lives is only crap because we have not truly come to grips with why we are going through something and we have failed to appreciate what we are meant to be learning. When we do begin to tackle it, we will be another step closer to fulfilling our true potential.

A positive attitude can be wonderfully useful! For example, a woman whose husband has betrayed her by being unfaithful and leaving her for another woman, is still left with a choice. She can continue to suffer agonies of bitterness and resentment for the rest of her life or, after the initial shock, she can turn it around. She can start to get herself back on her feet by saying, 'OK! I am *not* going to be destroyed by this. I have been a good wife and mother, and I can be strong for myself and the children. I *can* cope on my own. Nothing and nobody can make me negative – only I can do that!'

Life is often all about becoming tough in the positive sense of the word, of not allowing events and other people's mis-demeanours to crush or damage the good within us. 'I will survive' is one of the most positive, life-enhancing sentences there is, because contained within it is the acknowledgement that we are spiritual as well as physical beings who accept that everything in life, even painful experiences, has a purpose. This life may not be a bed of roses, but it is a purposeful continuum and it is not the end of our story!

I feel really strongly about the need for positive thoughts and life-enhancing affirmations. I love the impact of statements like, 'My life will be better from today' or 'I feel good, I can cope with this.' I have also learned, though, that we need to be very careful about what we ask for in life! A few years ago, I kept saying, 'I want a house', 'I want a house', 'I want a house in six months' time.' Eventually I got the house and I *hated* it. I now know that we have to phrase our wishes carefully. I should have been saying, 'I want a happy house', 'a good house', not just 'a house' – and if it was meant to be, if it was there in the blueprint of my life, I would have that happy house!

Perhaps the best way to deal with the 'why?' question is to change it to 'how?' Instead of saying, '*Why* is this happening to me?', we could say, '*How* can I begin to understand what is happening to me and resolve this situation?'

In the kind of work that I do, I often find myself being consulted as a kind of agony uncle, but an agony uncle who can hopefully bring an extra psychic dimension to any advice that's given. I recently became the resident psychic medium for a magazine entitled *Spiritual Lifestyle* and I now answer its readers' letters in a column headed 'Dear Tony . . .' Perhaps because she knew about this, a friend-of-a-friend, who was in very poor emotional shape, phoned me recently in floods of tears. When I eventually succeeded in getting her to say what was wrong, she blurted out, 'Please help me, Tony. I am *so* unhappy with my husband. He's no longer nice to me and now I've got a baby I can't go out to work and we are struggling to make ends meet all the time.'

'Darling,' I said, 'what's the chief problem with your husband?'

'He's not kind,' she replied. 'He never says nice things to me any more.'

'Do you say nice things to him?'

'No! Why should I? He's horrible.'

They had, I learned, been together for nineteen years and, by all accounts, he was not such a bad man.

'Darling,' I said, 'I get the sense that you really want this marriage to work.'

'Yes,' she replied. 'But I'm finding it too much of an uphill job at the moment.'

'Well, why not resolve to turn the situation around? Throughout the day, remember how much you used to love him and when he comes home tonight, when he comes through the door, tell him you still love him. Try to see things from his point of view. All your emotions are now engaged with the baby and, although this is a totally natural phase for a new mother, he's feeling very left out and frustrated, and he's resenting the fact that you no longer want him. If you want him to be kind and nice, darling, you need to be kind and nice, too. You need to explain that you are finding it difficult to be physically close with him right now because you are tired and because you feel he doesn't understand you or love you enough. But, in your heart of hearts, you *do* still love him and you *do* want to work it out and be happy again. Please just try. The moment he knows that you are still there for him; that the girl he fell in love with has not abandoned him; and that there's still a chance you can get back together again, things will change for the better.'

'But I really don't fancy him physically any more,' she confided.

'That's OK. We don't always have to fancy the people we love. We can love the spirit of the person, their essential goodness. What does it matter if he's become a bit of a podge, bless him. If you love him and he loves you, that's a great blessing. What you first appreciated about each other is what you need to get back to.'

I have no way of knowing whether that friend-of-a-friend took any notice of what I said, I just know that all her man needed to hear was that she was still there for him. At times, we all put up these guards and blame the other person, but a slight shift of emphasis can resolve a problem. If we are prepared to be honest with ourselves and lay our cards on the table, the other person is given the opportunity to see things from a different perspective, too. Such situations always remind me of that moment when President Kennedy said: 'Ask not what your country can do for you, but what you can do for your country'!

The truth is that 'no man is an island', and each of us has an impact on others. Being self-centred and on the make has one effect; being open and generous to those around us has another. We *can* change our ways, *can* empower ourselves to be positive rather than negative in our day-to-day life. When we stop saying 'why?' and change it to 'how?', we stop thinking of ourselves as victims and think of ourselves as victors! On a wet Sunday, when the weather is grim and grey and it is piddling down outside, instead of moaning and groaning we can think how cosy it will be to spend a day indoors and consider ways of making our home environment even lovelier while the rain replenishes the moisture in the ground for the plants and brings pleasure to the animals and the birds. It is in these simple ways that we turn life around. Affirmation is so important: 'I am going to be happy now' might begin just as words or a mantra, but there will come a time when we actually believe it and our life will start to change in the most mystical, dramatic ways.

Moderating any excessive behaviour or habitual views on life is always a good place to start. For example, I admit I swear like a trouper and I know I sound horrible when I do. The other night, a friend of mine, Angela, who is a very spiritual girl, reminded me of this and said, 'Tony, please don't keep swearing.'

'Oh, God, I'm *really* sorry to have upset you,' I said.

'I know you don't mean it,' she replied, 'and I know there's no malice in what you are saying, but remember that millions of people use swear words every day, and that every time those words are uttered in anger they carry a certain negative energy, vibration, along with them.'

I understood exactly what Angela was saying. Words have a ripple effect that can bring division or harmony. I cannot hold the belief that sacred words used in a spiritual chant or as mantras for meditation can do good in the world, while also believing that swear words, even when used without malice, carry no negative connotations or energy. Every thought, every word has an impact, and if I were to stop swearing that seemingly small effort would have an effect on the whole!

Likewise, we all have to be careful about the kind of influences we allow into our lives. Films, television, books and lyrics which glorify violence, killing and lust can have a major impact on minds, especially young, sensitive minds. I often recognise the effects of gross influences in my work. Vile things definitely have a negative influence on us, even if it just makes us more wary or nervous or less trusting of each other and of life itself. This impact takes on an even greater importance when we appreciate that the influences we take on board now can affect us for more than one lifetime!

'What happens to us after our physical bodies have ceased to function?' and 'How can we prepare ourselves for death?' are two questions that have fascinated human beings since the beginning of time, and both are relevant to the subject of good and bad influences in our lives. Preparing for death should never be a last-minute affair, but something we should be conscious of each and every day! The best way to prepare is by giving attention to how we are living and choosing to spend our allotted time in the here-and-now. This will affect how we treat others and the decisions we make in our day-to-day lives.

There are, of course, as many attitudes towards death and dying as there are people. Some of us, like the poet Dylan

Thomas, think of it as a fearsome event that should be resisted with all our might, and go along with the words of his poem, '*Do not go gentle into that good night . . . Rage, rage against the dying of the light.*' Others, like Robert Montgomery, welcome it as a friend:

> *There's nothing terrible in death;*
> *'Tis but to cast our robes away,*
> *And sleep at night, without a breath*
> *To break repose till dawn of day.*

As a child, I heard on a fairly regular basis that another kid's grandparent had died, and I used to find myself staring into space and wondering about death. 'How would it be,' I thought, 'if I just closed my eyes right now and died? Would there be nothing but a great black void?'

That thought never held any terrors for me. It just felt alien and I somehow *knew* that death was not like that. Now I can see that it was this belief that spurred me to look deeper into the mystery. I just could not accept that, once energy was created, it would become a nothing. What a waste! It simply had to go on, be transformed into something other.

I honestly cannot remember a time when I was frightened of death, because I knew that when my physical body ceased to be, my spirit would live on. Like most people who believe that death has no permanent sting, I understood the purpose and the value of this life in a very different way. People who believe in the afterlife no longer dread the future because they are too busy appreciating the importance of living in the present! Instead of fearing death, they acknowledge it as just another birth in which the spirit within us continues to another stage of its spiritual evolution.

So the best way to prepare for death is to appreciate the

wonder of life and live each day to the full, open ourselves up to good influences, and become as wise as we can in any one lifetime. Moving on, then, will be easy, just a matter of saying to our loved ones, 'Goodnight – God bless – see you soon!'

'Is it possible,' I am often asked, 'to contact everyone who has died?' – and sometimes people add something like, 'Can you contact Elvis for me?'

The answer in this instance is 'No'. That would only be possible if there was a direct connection between the person and Elvis – if, for example, the request was coming from a member of his family or a close friend. What draws a spirit to us is the link of love and the reassuring message they wish to bring to their loved ones or people who played an important role in their lives.

One example of this kind of communication was when a very well-turned-out, well-preserved American guy, who looked about sixty but who turned out to be seventy-five, came to me for a one-to-one reading. During the session, there was a sudden movement in my mind and I found myself looking directly into the face of the film star Lucille Ball. Doubting myself – and forgetting for a moment that it is often just a matter of getting one's doubts out of the way and letting the spirit people bring the information through – I was not at all sure whether it was really Lucille Ball or another glamorous woman with red hair who looked like her.

In the end, speaking in a rather apologetic tone, I said to the man, 'I'm really sorry, but all I can see is Lucille Ball standing between the two of us.'

'I'm not surprised,' he said. 'I was a great friend of hers when she was alive.'

I was so shocked that I forgot what I was supposed to be doing for a moment or two, but then I was able to give him

Lucille's loving reassurance that there was life after death. Having done this, she suddenly moved to one side and I found myself looking into the face of another film star, this time Rock Hudson.

'Oh, wow!' I said. 'Rock Hudson's here, too.'

'That's great,' the man said. 'I was a good friend of his, too.'

I was so pleased for this guy. He did not say much about the stars themselves, but I was left with the impression that he had worked with both of them.

On a more recent occasion, when I was doing a reading for a middle-aged guy, his mum and dad and other members of his family came through, but not his wife.

'She's not here,' I said, sad that he was disappointed. 'Tell me her name and I will try again.'

'Her name's Pat,' he replied.

In my mind, I was pleading, 'Come on, Pat, come in. Speak to him, darling.'

Empowered this time with her name, the spirit of his wife blended with my mind and gave me a most wonderful, but very personal message for him.

Nine times out of ten when mediums encounter this kind of problem, the spirit does eventually succeed in finding the link to the medium's mind. I do not know the cause of the initial difficulty, but I do know that sometimes a photograph or piece of jewellery that belonged to the spirit when they were alive can accelerate the connection.

So, no, we cannot communicate with everyone, but the majority of our loved ones do want to come back and say, 'Hi, I'm fine,' and just give some evidence that they are well and that they are there and watching over us. It really is a question of whether they feel there is a need to come and if they have the power and strength in them to make the link. If somebody has only recently passed over, it can be very difficult to get them to come through, and we have to wait a few months. Having said that, I have done some of my best readings when somebody has just died, so there is no general rule.

As a medium, it is too easy to fall into the trap of asking too much of oneself, to overdo things and get the measure wrong. But there has to be measure in everybody's work. For a long time, although I knew I should not do it, I used to push the limits every day and do too many readings or demonstrations, then get very depleted and feel ill. On one occasion I did over a hundred short readings in a day, and then I was ill for two days. This was at Alton Towers, the theme park in Staffordshire, when I was asked by *Living TV to chat to people in a marquee that had been set up for visitors who were interested in the paranormal.

The idea was that I should greet people and sign some autographs. The mistake I made occurred in the very first moment, because the first person who came up to me, pulled up a chair next to me, began to cry and said, 'Can I ask you a question about my child?' This naturally created a stir and, because I responded, a precedent! The next person also asked a question. Soon I had a queue and every person who sat down wanted a reading and received a message from a loved one.

After a while I knew I should get up and walk away from the marquee, but each time I looked at the next person in the queue, I could not bring myself to refuse them a message. So I continued, on and on, until I was burned out.

Success, I learned that day, can be as dangerous as failure. If you are a good medium, who avoids getting tangled up in your own ego, the messages will flow through you. But even so, measure is essential. Likewise, if the reading proves to be a difficult one, when, for example, the energy is all wrong because the person is not open to what I am trying to say to them, this can affect my energy because I so want it to be a life-enhancing experience for them. As time goes by, though, I am becoming wiser. Occasionally, I now say, 'Darling, I can't do this for you right now, but don't be despondent, tomorrow is another day.'

One of the really positive things to come out of the Alton Towers weekend, though, was that I got to spend some time with the medium Derek Acorah and his wife Gwen. Derek is the star of the TV programme *Most Haunted*, and although by then I had worked with him a few times, there had not really been any time for us to socialise. During this weekend, however, we were able to relax together over dinner and a few drinks at the hotel. I really enjoyed that and I am looking forward to working with Derek again in the future.

Looking back, I can see that all those years spent working in accounts departments and part-time as a medium, were years in which I concentrated on laying down a solid spiritual foundation by reading all the spiritual books I could lay my hands on. This period satisfied my passion for the paranormal and gave me a wealth of knowledge and understanding, which stood me in good stead for the future.

In 1998 I did something fairly radical. I decided the time had come for a change and, as I wanted to stay closer to home so that I could devote more time to my spiritual development, I applied for a totally different kind of job. Having got it, my heart leapt with joy and I began work as a wedding planner for a hotel in Essex.

Working out the details for a happy couple's big day was much more fun than doing a company's accounts, and I was now really enjoying both aspects of my work – the bread-and-butter and the spiritual. That, I thought, was change and blessing enough.

But I was about to discover that there is truth in one of my favourite sayings. God, really does work in mysterious ways His wonders to perform. Four-and-a-half years later, in 2002, there was another change in store for me – one that would change my life and hurtle me into a totally different world!

7
Up in Lights

I first met Colin Fry, who's blessed with the ability to give remarkable messages from the spirit world, at a seminar when I was nineteen. Over the years, we often met on professional occasions and did demonstrations together. Colin has always worked tirelessly to bring messages from people's loved ones, and I was very pleased for him when I heard that he had been approached by International Programme Marketing (IPM), a television production company, to make a series of programmes called *6ixth Sense* for *Living TV, and that he was getting some very good reviews.

By 2002, having started my own spiritual work at the age of nineteen, I had been working as a clairvoyant for fourteen years. During this time I had done countless one-to-one readings and stage demonstrations, and also been involved in taking development groups and seminars. Stuart and I had also co-founded a group called the Avalon Project, to promote mediumistic and spiritual learning. The idea behind this is to offer people who are interested in studying the paranormal the opportunity to meet some of the world's most amazing tutors and demonstrators. Even more important, the Avalon Project creates support groups for those who are just beginning their spiritual journey and who needed opportunities to share their thoughts and experiences on a one-to-one basis or at resident seminars and one-day workshops.

Having achieved my ambition to be a psychic medium,

albeit only on a part-time basis, I was perfectly content and would have been happy to continue working in this vein for the remainder of my days. From about the age of thirty-two, however, I had started to receive some rather mysterious messages from the spirit world.

'Your name,' the voices were telling me, 'is going to be up in lights!'

I felt quite unsettled by this. In the past I had had enough trouble with my nerves getting in the way of the work, and the last thing I wanted now was anything that would put me in a situation where I was out of my depth.

Nobody was listening to my worries and concerns, though, and behind the scenes, life was unravelling other plans for me!

'International Programme Marketing,' Colin Fry informed me one afternoon, 'is looking for another medium to do some clairvoyant/psychic programmes with a different edge from my programme, and the company wants a younger person, preferably a bloke, who has a sense of humour.'

Well, there are not that many to choose from in our field, and Colin, bless him, had told them about me!

When Hilary Goldman, IPM's executive producer, telephoned, her first question was: 'Are you working now – and if so, can we come and see you in action?'

It just so happened that, three days later, I was booked to do a demonstration in the Broadway Theatre, Lewisham, and I suggested that this would be a good opportunity for her to come along.

I must confess I was very nervous on the evening of her visit, but once I'd calmed myself down and reminded myself that everything was in the lap of the gods, all went well. The audience, although in a somewhat rowdy mood, was receptive, and I was able to do some really sound readings, which people were happy to confirm. Afterwards, as I was walking

Hilary to her car, she said that she had really enjoyed the demonstration and liked the way I worked.

'Would you like to do a pilot?' she asked me.

Now I know this will sound naïve, but at that time my only understanding of the word 'pilot' was as the form of address for a guy who flew aeroplanes. I hadn't a clue that the term was also used for the making of a programme that was then shown to television executives in the hope that they would cough up some money and commission a series. Despite my ignorance, though, I had already given up resisting the spirits and I knew that I had to say yes to whatever Hilary suggested! By then I knew that Hilary, her husband Craig, also an executive producer at IPM, and their team had a great attitude to working with mediums. Their knowledge and understanding of paranormal subjects was second to none, and they had great respect for the mediums who worked with them.

Mediums who work on TV are often portrayed by the media in a less than favourable light, so agreeing to work on TV was a little scary for me. I soon discovered, however, that I felt safe working with Hilary and Craig, and it was great being with the same company as Colin Fry, who had always been so supportive of my work.

A couple of weeks later, I found myself in Hilary's beautiful house in the leafy suburbs of Loughton, Essex, doing an afternoon demonstration for twenty Jewish ladies. Also present was a five-man camera crew.

The group of ladies, I soon discovered, were a fantastic bunch – warm, generous and open – and having, as they said, 'taken to me', they were all willing me to do well and impress the programme makers. Not surprisingly in these circumstances, I made some very nice contacts with the spirit world, and the spirits brought forward some detailed pieces of information about relatives of those present who had died and how it had happened. It was very emotional at times and a few tears were shed that afternoon.

This was the first time I had been in front of a TV camera, but once I started work I discovered I did not think about the camera, the lights, the sound-recording equipment, the crew or the maze of trailing wires. I was too focused on the readings to worry about any of that. This is how it is with mediumship: you enter an altered state of mind and being, where you are so focused on other-worldly matters that the last thing you worry about is what is happening in this world.

The pilot that was made that day was then shown to the executives at *Living TV, which describes itself as the 'Home of the Paranormal'.

When Hilary and Craig telephoned me, it was good news. '*Living TV *loves* the pilot,' they told me. 'And they *really* liked you. They hated the shirt you were wearing, though, and said you would really need to do something about your hair!'

'Right,' I said, trying to remember which shirt I had worn and how my hair had looked that day, '*right*!'

With these comments off their chest, the *Living TV execs had apparently commissioned another paid-for pilot, which Hilary and Craig decided should be filmed partly in Loughton High Street and partly in the Lakeside shopping centre in Essex.

The idea for the programme, which was called *Street Psychic*, was that I should go out on the street, trailed by a camera crew, and randomly approach passers-by – all complete strangers. Having introduced myself as a psychic, I would then ask them if I could do a one-to-one reading for them.

Prior to filming the programme, I was informed that the Independent Television Corporation (ITC) had very strict rules about paranormal matters and mediumship and would not allow any 'talking to dead people', because members of the

Corporation did not believe in it and they were determined to safeguard the sanity of the nation! What I would have to do instead was concentrate my psychic abilities on the living and determine whether or not the people I met were married, if they had children, where they went on holiday, and then hopefully add some significant info about their past or future.

On the first day of filming, at Lakeside on a warm, sunny day in August, I was absolutely terrified. Kitted out with a pair of blue jeans, black shoes and a shirt that everybody approved of, I felt OK in the clothes, but completely out of my depth. Directed to walk into the shopping mall and stop someone – anyone – I then introduced myself by saying, 'Hello, I'm Tony Stockwell. I'm a clairvoyant working with *Living TV and I'd like to give you a reading.'

I might as well have said 'a punch on the nose' or a 'dose of arsenic'! Some members of the public were outright hostile, some just plain sceptical, while the majority backed away from me and scurried off. No one, it seemed, wanted a reading, and the crew heard me cry: 'Let's get outta here!'

I was not really surprised, though. I had a big camera crew in tow – about thirteen people altogether – and I think most of the shoppers thought I was going to ask them to test a brand of margarine or washing powder, or worse, set them up for some kind of *Candid Camera* or *You've Been Framed* sketch. Eventually, after much huffing and puffing and many rejections, a few kind people did take pity on me and stopped. Then, amid gasps of surprise, I gave them information about themselves, and had some lovely connections which did not contravene the ITC regulations.

On the first of these occasions, I instantly picked up that the lady I was reading for had been seriously messed about by the men in her life, and that she was now very wary and suspicious of any man who tried to get close to her. In her heart of hearts, however, she regretted that she was the only person among her friends who had never married, and she longed to be more trusting. In fact, the thought that occupied her mind most was: 'When will it be my turn?' I also picked up on the fact that one of her ex-lovers had been in the habit of stealing money from her, and that one of her closest friends was currently in a very abusive relationship. This lady, my first *Street Psychic* volunteer, was very responsive and obviously quite overwhelmed by the accuracy of the detail.

I informed the next young man, who said he was 'up' for a reading, that he had a musical talent. He then confirmed on camera that he played two instruments, the piano and the trumpet.

The next young lady willing to have a reading also confirmed what I told her.

'Yes,' she said, astonished, 'my grandmother has hurt the left side of her body – and, yes, she does have a mobility problem. She fell out of a car, damaged her knee and has been in pain ever since.'

Another of my obliging volunteers was discovered in a hairdresser's, and I immediately homed in on the fact that this lady was more often up in the air than on land. She was, I said, a much travelled person, who had a very strong sense of adventure and who would continue to fly on a regular basis.

'I'm an air stewardess,' she confirmed, laughing!

All in all we gathered sufficient material from the Lakeside and Loughton readings for IPM to make a one-hour programme that went down very well with *Living TV. A further six one-hour episodes were then commissioned and were filmed in Canterbury, Brighton, Norwich, Southend on Sea and London, and perhaps because I was now in my stride we met with much less hostility and resistance from the passers-by.

Just as we were coming to the end of shooting *Street Psychic*, Hilary said she thought it would be a really good follow-up if we were to train other people – ordinary members of the public – to be psychics. She suggested that this programme could be called *Psychic School* and I could be the teacher!

As I have always believed that everybody has some psychic powers, to a greater or lesser degree I, thought this was a fascinating idea that would make excellent viewing.

To get the programme off the ground, IPM placed an advertisement at the end of one of its other psychic TV programmes: *Do you think you are psychic? Would you like the opportunity to be trained by one of the country's leading mediums? If so, telephone this number.*

The response was overwhelming – about 8,000 telephone calls! These were then whittled down by asking people to tell us why they felt they were psychic and what paranormal experiences they had had in the past. About 200 people were then selected and interviewed at *Living TV's offices over two days. The would-be psychics were given a series of tests, such as being blindfolded and told to describe a person in the centre of the room just by sensing the emotions emanating from them. They also had to reveal the colour of a piece of fabric with their eyes closed. The selectors' panel consisted of Richard Woolfe (the commissioning editor), Colin Fry and myself, and over a period of several days we whittled the finalists down to ten people.

As part of the wanna-be psychics' training, we took our chosen ten – five men and five women – to Castle Stuart in Inverness, which is situated in a magnificent setting on the Moray Firth in the Scottish Highlands. We could not have chosen a better venue. Having entered its portals, you can walk the same battlements that Charles I trod before he lost his kingdom and his head, and that Bonnie Prince Charlie stepped out onto the night before his tragic defeat at nearby Culloden Moor.

The castle, not surprisingly given its rich history, has a reputation for being haunted. '*Are you brave enough to hear about the Three-Turret Haunted Bedroom at the top of the East Tower?*', its literature asks.

This room is where a local poacher known as Big Angus, who was said to be afraid of neither man nor beast, was recorded to have risked spending the night in order to prove to the Earl of Moray that the castle was not haunted and to earn the twenty-pound reward that was on offer from the minister at Petty Church. The reward was to remain unclaimed. The next morning, poor Angus's body was found in the courtyard, a look of horror frozen on his face. He was long dead, and the mystery – and the ghost of Big Angus – remains to haunt the castle to this very day!

A ghost, I believe, is a spirit who remains walking about earth because they still have a strong emotional attachment to a building or a place, or because they are left feeling they still have something to accomplish here. The extraordinary thing is that quite often when I ask people if they believe in life after death, they say, 'No'. But when I ask them if they believe in ghosts, they say, 'Yes'! This strikes me as an obvious contradiction, but I have come to the conclusion that some people find the belief in ghosts a lot easier and less challenging to accept than a belief in the afterlife!

Poltergeist activity – when a ghostly spirit manifests its presence by rapping on surfaces or making other noises, and by acts of mischief, such as moving objects or throwing furniture around – certainly does occur, and this may well be the handiwork of an emotionally-disturbed ghost who is going through a period of adjustment after death.

I myself have witnessed the movement of objects in a room, but this has always been the work of playful spirits rather than disturbing poltergeist activity. I remember an occasion with Arthur Clarke, a medium who died some years ago. Inexplicable things always seemed to happen around Arthur and, one day, when we were sitting in a group in the humble setting of a converted garage in Rainham, Essex, a jug of water rose off the table and into the air, touched the ceiling and came gently down to rest on the table again. It was not at all scary. On the contrary, it was thrilling – exciting – because we knew it was the work of a playful spirit energy.

The plan, while we were at Castle Stuart, was to see if our students could pick up on the castle's vibes and unearth any of its resident ghosts, and also to do a ghost-busting sequence in Culloden, where I was to have that amazing experience with the young clansman, Andrew. We also planned to cover meditation, how to be a clairvoyant, pendulum work and detecting spirit orbs.

Once at the castle, I set about getting the students in the right frame of mind so that they could open up to the spirit world. I must say they did incredibly well at picking up the vibes of the castle and its grounds, and also those of a nearby burial place, which dated back to 2000BC. On the first night, Michelle, one of the students, was in bed when she felt the presence of a little girl by her side who kept trying to lift her up by the arm. On another night she saw the same girl again in a room which had once been a nursery.

During our stay, we were also blessed by a visit from Angela Tarry, an aura expert from Sussex, who arrived carrying an unusual piece of kit. Angela had travelled up to Scotland to spend a few hours with the *Psychic School* students and to photograph their energy fields.

'The camera I am holding,' she explained, 'gives a very good representation of the auric field, which is the energy field that exists all around us. This relates to our physical, emotional and spiritual being. Usually when we see an aura, the strongest part of it is from the waist upwards, and although it goes right round our bodies, it is weaker at the bottom. We don't know why this is. Basically the camera is quite simple. The film goes in at the back and there is a very small viewfinder. People look through this and put their hands on the two handplates which read the vibrations. A colour then oscillates at a frequency that is read by the plates, so it's a bio feedback. This image then goes into the camera and the camera translates it into a Polaroid photo.'

Before she photographed the students, Angela tried out the camera on me, and she was very surprised when a third of the picture was covered by a mysterious white area and failed to appear.

'This is very spooky,' Angela said.

'Maybe the energy in the castle is affecting it,' I replied. 'It is a very haunted place.'

'Yes, there's certainly a lot of spiritual energy around. Look, here is some evidence on your right shoulder of the presence of somebody whispering in your ear. I think your heart has really opened up this week because you have loved what you've been doing. It's been a real kick for you and you have moved into a much deeper place than you were in before you came here.'

'Yes,' I agreed. 'I've really enjoyed the whole experience.'

The first student who had his auric photograph taken was Seylan. Angela, who knew nothing about his background, then used the photograph to help him to see how far he had come in his spiritual development.

'This side of the photograph,' she explained, 'represents emotional energy – what is going on inside you, how you express yourself in the world. And this – right at the top – is your spiritual energy coming in. So it is obvious that there has been a complete change in the way that you think about things this week.'

'Yes,' Seylan replied. 'I have definitely changed in the way I notice and react to things. Number one on the list is that before, when I was around certain people, I closed myself off from them. But having Craig in the group, the first gay guy I have ever really interacted with, has opened me up, made me see things very differently.'

Angela then worked her way through the other students and each, thanks to the auric camera, learned something new about him or herself.

Late one evening, just as a heavy fog was starting to settle outside, we drove the students to the area where the Battle of Culloden had taken place in 1746 and, having had a rather bizarre picnic on the cold, damp moor, we set about sensing the terrible violence and traumatic events that had taken place there. Having split the group into two, I took charge of one and placed Michelle in charge of the other. I then took my lot off to the north and Michelle took hers off to the east.

As Michelle's group headed deeper into the forest, they unwittingly made for the spot where the worst slaughter of the Scottish clansmen had taken place and, unaware of their location, stopped precisely at the point where hundreds of clansmen were mown down by English firepower.

Sales manager Craig was the first to feel the pain of the battle.

'Someone has just stabbed me in the back and is still digging the knife in me now,' he gasped. 'My head is being held back.'

'I can feel something trickling down my back,' another of the students exclaimed. 'I think it's blood. I'm experiencing a lot of pain, a lot of anger, and there are spirits here who can't move on. It feels like an ambush, a trap. I'm surrounded. There's a lot of stuff here and none of it is good.'

A quarter of a mile away, my group had stumbled on a monument that marked the grave of the fallen. While we were in that slightly-off-the-beaten-track area, I asked my group to form a circle, and it was not long before the students began to pick up on the vibes of the brutal Battle of Culloden.

Kevin, an ex-policeman, experienced a violent blow from a highland warrior's axe. Hit on the back of the head, he was cleavered right through his skull by a blow that plunged down as far as his shoulders. He was also struck under his right ribcage with a claymore, which again laid him open, and he experienced further panic when his femur was broken, his leg was trapped and he couldn't move.

Irene visibly shuddered and said that she felt as if she was dying and could sense the presence of horses all around her.

Looking back, I think we felt so much more when we were off the beaten track because the spirit energy was still preserved there. On the more commonly used tourist tracks, much of this had already been stripped away by the vibes left by sightseers.

When we reached base, I asked Michelle how her group had got on.

'It's been a fantastic experience for them,' she said, 'one that I think will change their lives forever. One of the group felt a soldier lying on the ground. He was very badly injured, knew it was all over, didn't want to stay there like that, and was pleading, *begging* with a friend to help him end his life. The student could feel the strength of their friendship, and the bonds between them were so strong that the man was able to do as his friend asked and take his life.'

Back at the castle, Craig, who had felt himself taken back in time to the battle and had felt a sword being run right through him, was experiencing so much pain he needed a healing session. Michelle also told me that, as she was leading her group on the moor, she had heard a great rumbling, just like thunder, and that this had been accompanied by the sound of thousands of people running.

It was all very dramatic and there was absolutely no doubt that the students' experiences that night were very real.

On one occasion while we were filming in the castle, we found ourselves in a big ballroom that had many small turreted rooms leading off it. Part of this sequence included me leading the students around the room at night to see if they could pick up any emanations or memories of things that had happened there in the past. I was in for a surprise!

In one tiny room that I entered, I had the sense of a little boy, whose legs were badly crippled, trying to lift himself up to the window so that he could look below and feel himself to be a part of the life beyond. I then also picked up that he was the son of the master of the castle and that his father considered him a disgrace – a blight on the family's good name – because he was a cripple.

Without saying a word to the students about what I had sensed, I asked them to go into the room one by one. On their return, several of them spoke of having had a similar experience to the one I had had. 'My legs felt funny'; 'I felt as if I was a child'; 'I was a child struggling to look out of the window'.

Using our minds, we then lifted the child from that dark space into the light. And, as we did so, I allowed him to come close to me. Then, taking on his persona, I said silently, 'Darling, you don't need to be here any longer. Your legs are perfect in spirit. You can go forward into the light and be healed.'

There was then this marvellous sense of him being rescued – lifted out of that turret room and going forward.

By the time our visit to Castle Stuart ended, we had enough material to make five one-hour programmes of *Psychic School* for *Living TV, and I particularly enjoyed the write-up by Graeme Donohoe in the Scottish edition of the *Sun* on 19 June 2003. Donohoe had attended the press event that we'd organised after the visit, and under the heading 'Turning the tables – *Sun* man gets positive vibe in Psychic School', he wrote:

A rickety wooden table starts to rock backwards, as my eyes stare intently at Tony Stockwell's hands to see if he's pushing it. Tony is just fresh from filming *Psychic School* for *Living TV at ancient Castle Stuart, near Inverness, and has invited the Scottish *Sun* to take part in one of his classes.

'Come on, sweetie, rock the table. Come on, show us what you can do,' coaxes Tony, as three hardened journos wonder if we've been invited to Psycho School!

The table starts to rock, but the cynic in me is convinced that Tony's at it. He steps completely away from the object of our attention and – surprise, surprise – the rocking begins to slow till it eventually comes to a halt.

'Don't do this to me, sweetie. Please move,' pleads an exasperated Tony.

Suddenly, the table begins to jolt back to life again, and this time Tony's hands are nowhere near it.

The rocking motion speeds up and to my amazement the table starts to lurch in a clockwise direction.

Soon it is virtually impossible to keep our fingertips on the table as it starts spinning uncontrollably around the room. We all laugh our heads off, struggling to take in what's going on, when eventually the table sends us crashing into the wall and stops dead.

How on earth did that just happen? This psychic stuff is surely a lot of nonsense for weak-minded fools?

Before now the only spirits I'd have said could move things around the room would be vodka and tequila – and I'm at a complete loss to explain the incredible moving table.

'Sometimes the spirits just like to have a bit of fun,' Tony reveals. 'Before now I've had a huge marble table levitate fully off the ground . . .'

The jury is still out on the psychic phenomenon and *Psychic School*. But after being baffled by a table that seemed to be auditioning for a part in *The Exorcist*, I can only hope the court bench is nailed down when the verdict is reached.

The ghosts at Castle Stuart were not the only ghosts I encountered that year. When Hilary and Craig gave a launch party at their house for *Street Psychic*, I met a young neighbour of theirs who I had also met previously. On the first occasion, the woman had told me that her family and some of their friends all felt that there was something very sinister going on in one particular room of her house.

'Could you possibly go in there to see if you can pick up anything?', she asked me at the time.

It was not a good moment for me to be asked such a thing! We had been filming all day and my energies were at a rather low ebb, but I agreed to do what she asked. When I entered the room, I was immediately aware of a presence and, a couple of minutes later, having thought that I had dealt with the matter for her, I came back out and said cheerfully, 'Don't worry, darling, all's well in there now.'

That wishful thinking came back to haunt me some months later when we met again at the launch party.

'You know that room you visited before,' she said. 'The strange atmosphere is back again. Could you possibly come round to the house after the party and see what else you can pick up?'

'Of course,' I said. 'Stuart and I will come back with you when the party finishes.'

So Stuart and I accompanied the lady to her house and entered the room that she was so concerned about. As we did so, both of us sensed the presence of a young boy, aged about fourteen, and, without saying a word to each other, we found ourselves drawn to an upstairs room that was situated just under the eaves. Once we were in that room, we both had a strong impression that this was the boy's bedroom and that when he had lived in the house he had often played here. While in the room, Stuart picked up on two initials.

Later, some neighbours confirmed that the previous owners had had two sons, and that the initials Stuart had come up with were the initials of one of the boy's names. They also confirmed that this boy was aged fourteen when he had died in the house.

Neither Stuart nor I felt that there was any need to move the boy's spirit on. We simply asked him not to alarm the new residents by making his presence obvious. To my knowledge, he has not!

All places have ambiences – and occasionally some have a sense of evil. As a sensitive I can tune into the atmosphere of a room and I might, for example, be able to tell you that twenty-five years ago there was a murder committed in there. This is hardly surprising when you think about it. Every old house has a history, and at one time or another someone is sure to have been born or died there. The vibes of these experiences are present for sensitives to connect with. Such presences manifest in different parts of my body, sometimes the back of my head, sometimes my neck or shoulders, sometimes as a pulling sensation in my stomach. Sometimes I also sense something damp, wet and grey leaning against me. This may not be a spirit person; it may simply be the atmosphere of a place.

It is always essential, though, when people talk about evil spirits and evil places, to keep a sense of perspective. On one occasion, a young girl came to me after a demonstration and said that she thought she was psychic.

'Horrible spirits visit me in the dead of night and wake me up,' she told me, 'They sit on my chest and I can smell their foul breath in my face.'

People who experience such awful things are not always deluded or fanciful, but many – especially those whose mind-set is geared towards the negative – may attract negative energies, or even convince themselves that unreal things are happening to them.

Our kind of work is prone to attracting some rather negative and totally misguided people. It is an occupational hazard, but we have our own way of dealing with it. At one demonstration, for example, a lady managed to enter the venue with a can of paraffin and matches. Apparently, she was going to light up the place and take us all to heaven. Luckily the organiser bounced her out!

I guess nobody can really prepare a person for the phenomenal difference that being seen on TV can make to life, and I was totally unprepared for the impact that *Street Psychic* and *Psychic School* had on mine.

The transmission of these two programmes, accompanied by the usual hype and publicity associated with appearing on TV, completely changed my life. Instead of me sidling up to passers-by in streets and shopping malls, strangers now approached me, and wherever I walked or whatever train I travelled on, my face was often recognised. Everybody was so friendly and supportive that my self-confidence soared – and people's reactions made it much easier for me to trust that this new direction in my work was what the spirits had been foretelling for some time. My name *was* now lit up in TV credits and in hoardings outside theatre venues!

I knew then that it was time for another change in my life. Much as I loved the glamorous world of wedding planning, I was finding it increasingly difficult to dovetail this and all the new offers of work that were coming in, including the opportunity to go to America and film another *Street Psychic*, this time a special which was to be called *Street Psychic in San Francisco*, and to make guest appearances on Colin Fry's *6ixth Sense*. Only too aware which way the spirits wished me to go, I decided to give up my day job as a wedding planner and forge ahead with the spiritual work.

As soon as I had done this and totally dedicated myself to working with the spirits, I found myself wondering why I had not done it before. Now, in addition to being on TV and giving public demonstrations, private readings, and teaching in workshops and seminars, I was inundated with offers to do still more TV work and bigger stage demonstrations and tours, including a tour of South Africa and the US. My work as a psychic medium was now more than a full-time job, it was the equivalent of two jobs, and, hectic as it was, I could not have been happier!

Before I was on TV, I used to get an audience of about 150 people when I was doing a local demonstration, but recently 600 people turned up for 300 seats! And this very week I have given demonstrations for 5,000 people over the course of three days. In the early days, people were always saying to me: 'Be careful, Tony, don't let it go to your head', but I have kept my feet firmly on the ground and my ego has not got the better of me.

*　　*　　*

So in June 2003 I found myself in the US filming *Street Psychic in San Francisco*. This proved to be a fantastic experience, both from a work and a time-off point of view, because I had sufficient free time between the filming of the various readings to play tourist and visit the sights.

On one of my free days I caught a ferry over to the notorious Alcatraz prison, now the 'star' of many films, and which welcomes thousands of tourists every day. Having decided to do the prison tour, I hired the headphones and listened to the commentary that guides you around the awesome-looking place and also recreates some of the sound-effects of when the prison was still functional. As I was listening, I suddenly became aware of a terrifying sense of foreboding and the blackest of black depressions and feelings of hopelessness. These sensations, which were not at all pleasant, totally caught me off guard and, ripping off the headphones as fast as I could, I hurried out of the building to escape the terrible feelings. Looking back, I am not sure if I had picked up on the vibes of one particular inmate who was now in spirit, or if I'd simply connected with the collective left-over energy of the place. All I know is that it was an exceedingly unpleasant experience.

A few weeks before we were due to leave for San Francisco, I kept being made aware of the spirit of the film star Diana Dors, the platinum blonde pin-up girl. Her face would appear before me, and she would call out her name, laugh, then disappear. This must have happened at least six times, and I kept wondering why.

A short time later, when I was in a bar in San Francisco with some of the American film crew, Diana Dors came to me again. This time, the vision of her was even clearer than it had been before, and she didn't only call out her name. Pointing to the other end of the bar, she said proudly, 'My picture is on that wall.' I was so thrown by this that my face must have been a picture, too!

Having explained to the crew what had just happened, we all went to the other end of the bar to examine the wall that Diana had pointed out. It was, we discovered, full of pictures of movie stars, but they were all current stars like Cameron Diaz, Tom Cruise and Nicole Kidman, so I felt it was very unlikely that we would find a picture of a 1950's star. After scanning the photos for about ten minutes, however, right in the top corner we found a tiny, obviously very ancient, signed photograph of Diana. She was right – there she was on that wall!

I was really pleased to read for San Franciscans. The vibes of the city were relaxed and cosmopolitan and, on the whole, the people were open and remained very approachable, even when they realised they were being talked to by a man from another country who was professing to be a psychic and asking to read for them.

At this time, the strict ITC regulation about mediumship and the contacting of spirits on TV were relaxed, so when filming this show I was able to pass on messages from people's loved ones, rather than just giving readings about their current lives and relationships.

I began the filming by asking an assortment of passers-by if they believed in psychics. The answers were as varied as the people themselves.

'I think there are a lot of fake psychics and mediums out there, but there is the very rare person who may be able to pick up on something.'

'Absolute phonies! They don't know what they're talking about.'

'Well, people of San Francisco are very receptive. I call this the last liberal enclave.'

'Most San Franciscans are too smart for psychics.'

'To be a psychic you have to have an after-death experience.'

'I don't believe in God, so I can't believe in psychics.'

'It's kind of spooky, really, when some of it comes true.'

'Maybe there is some sort of supernatural power in all of us.'

As I was walking around, a member of the crew asked me if I could feel any vibes about San Francisco, and I had to explain that in places visited by lots of people, in this case tourists, the energy became saturated by their vibes! I found it quite upsetting at one level that modern life had overpowered so much of the energy of the days gone by. San Francisco has one of the most amazing histories of anywhere in the world. John Sutter first discovered gold there in 1848 and people flocked to the city from all round the world to make their fortunes. Nearly half a billion dollars' worth of gold was hauled from the ground, and the descendants of the original gold-diggers still populate the city.

Walking along the sidewalk, speaking to camera, I said:

'Hi, and welcome to a very special edition of *Street Psychic*, coming to you from San Francisco. I can't believe we're here. It's apparently one of the most open-minded cities in America, but we are soon going to find out. I am doing what I usually do, giving readings to people on the street. Hopefully, these people are going to want to stop and speak to me today. God knows what we will find. America is the land of the free, and San Francisco is about as free as you can get – *free* love, *free* speech and *free* mediumistic readings. Now you can't argue with that. Can you?'

The next moment I spotted a lady in a jeweller's shop and I made a beeline for her.

'Darling,' I said, coming to a halt beside her, 'have you got two seconds? Do you believe in psychics?'

'Yes, I do,' she replied, startled.

'Well, I am one. I'm making a programme for the UK. Would you be up for a reading?'

'Sure – great.'

'What's your name?' I asked as we shook hands.

'Heather.'

'I'm Tony. I'll do my best to give you an accurate psychic reading. We'll see what we can do.'

Having closed my eyes, I began: 'Heather, I've got a very strong sense of a male energy that wants to come between you and me. As this man comes close to me, I get a definite sense that, although he knew he was destined not to be long in this world, the end of his life was rather sudden and came quicker than he thought. But there was a definite lead-up before he passed. This man was loved, he had a good family around him; he was adored. As he comes close to me I get a pain in my head, I feel slightly dizzy, and there is something here to do with blood and blood tests.'

'Oh my God!' Heather gasped, raising her hand to her mouth. 'You're talking about my ex-husband.'

'Are you OK?'

'Yes.'

'All I know is that there is a man between you and me. As he comes in, this man is talking about his head and the dizziness. Did he enjoy a drink in life?'

'Yes.'

'OK, we all enjoy a drink, but I think he maybe enjoyed a little too much drink from time to time, and that he could be a little violent and aggressive in his life.'

'Yes,' Heather said, beginning to weep.

'This man wants to apologise. He's come here to say that

he's sorry because he knows he spoke to you unkindly and treated you badly before he passed over. Are you OK with that?'

'Yes, yes,' she said, dabbing her eyes.

'It may have been seven years before he passed. Can you think back that length of time?'

'Yes. Yes.'

'You kind of distanced yourself from him seven years before he passed? There was some kind of separation?' I paused as she nodded. 'Do you have two children?'

'Yes. Those were his children.'

'OK, he is now talking to me about loving two kids. He is coming to you with a great deal of love, but he also wants to talk about the kids that he loved. It's important for him to bring back a message to these children that he is well, that he is fine.' I paused again. 'Do you know a gentleman who died in a car accident, or a road accident? Do say no if you don't.'

'Not offhand.'

'Then who is David?'

Heather gasped, leaning back on the wall behind her. 'David's my ex-husband's brother. He was in a very serious car accident. But he survived.'

'So maybe your ex-husband is acknowledging the fact that he has a brother and that he wants . . .' I paused, listening again. 'Jonathan? John? Who is that?'

'John,' Heather gasped again, 'is my new fiancé.'

'Does your John – or his father – know anyone who was in prison?'

'John's father,' Heather said, after a moment's pause, 'was paralysed and in a VA hospital for fourteen years before he died. He always described his condition as being "in prison".'

'This man had a medal that was kept? Is that true?'

'Yes.' The tears were running down Heather's face.

'John seems to be the third major relationship in your life. Third time lucky? Are you with me on this?'

'Yes. Oh, yes!'

'I really do feel that John will be your third-time-lucky in life and that, from this moment on, you will find a degree of contentment.' I paused, then added, 'I think this is pretty much what I need to tell you. God bless you. Thank you very much for listening to me.'

'Thank you – bye . . .' Heather sobbed as I brought the reading to an end.

A short time after we left Heather, we thought we would check out one of the oldest bars on Fisherman's Wharf. Inside, sitting at a table, I noticed a man and three women, and I decided I would like to do a reading for the man. He was very sceptical when I first approached him, but, after a little persuasion, he agreed to be filmed.

'I am aware of a gentleman here,' I began. 'This gentleman knew that he was passing before he passed; this man had some kind of ongoing illness before he went over. This same gentleman lost a lot of weight before he died. He was skinny and very frail before he went over.' I paused, listening intently to the spirit. 'What a nice guy, what a lovely, lovely man he is; this man is laughing and joking. It seems to me that there were five people who really adored him, five people who made a special effort to be with him during his last days, who made a special effort to make a vigil at his bedside at the end of his life. Five strong characters who he absolutely adored in life.'

Later, Gordon, the man I was reading for, said to camera: 'When Tony first started talking about a person who'd passed into the spirit world, and his illness before he was dying, that kind of got our attention because we – the four of us present – had just done a toast to a very dear friend of ours who had passed away within the last year.'

'This gentleman I am talking about,' I continued, 'is now telling me that he was a single man who had no children and, as he had no family of his own, he made his friends his family.'

I could sense the group exchanging astonished glances and nodding their heads in agreement. The next moment I heard myself asking the man: 'Your mother passed with a brain disease? I now have a lady here calling "Mum", and she's talking about her head, and the problems she had with her head before she died. She's saying it affected her for ten years before she died, and that she'd wished in some ways that she had died before she did. It seems to me that she lived a half-life towards the end of her life and this was very hard for her.'

Throughout this part of the reading, I could see the man weeping, but I had to continue because so much information was still flowing through for him.

'It was not only hard for her,' I added, 'but for everyone around her, too. She had to have a lot of nursing and other people coming into her home to help her before she died. There was a man who collected her in the spirit world. My feeling is that he was a younger man. She loved him, he loved her, and they were really pleased to get back together. It took her some time to adjust to where she was in the spirit world because when she passed she felt very confused, disorientated. But now she's back to her normal self. She's fit again and that's what she wants to tell you.'

Gordon, who had started out so sceptical and who was now feeling very emotional, confirmed the details of this part of the reading on camera. 'My mother died of Alzheimer's,' he said. 'She really suffered and probably did wish she could have died five years before she did. It's *not* a good way to go. My mum had a dearly loved brother who passed away many years before her when he was of college age. He died in an automobile accident. After my mother passed away, we found a very loving letter addressed to her from her brother – the love of a brother for a sister love-letter, if that makes sense. We knew that she had always had a deep love for her brother and that she missed him immensely throughout her whole life. Tony was spot on,' he added. 'I was very impressed with his reading. He nailed some stuff that made me believe him.'

I was so pleased. Like a lot of blokes, Gordon had started out not believing, but by the end I think I'd managed to persuade him that I was not a fraudster.

A few minutes after we had left the bar on Fisherman's Wharf, I found myself approaching two ladies, a mother and a daughter, who were sitting sunning themselves on a wall.

'Do you believe in psychics?' I asked.

'Yes,' they replied in unison.

'My name is Tony, may I sit on the wall next to you? Your name,' I said to the mother, 'is?'

'Crystal.'

'And your name is?'

'Catherine,' the daughter replied.

'I'll do a reading for you, Crystal. I hope it's good for you. Please be honest with me and tell me "yes" or "no", whether you understand it or not.

'I have a lady here,' I began, 'who had a cancer when she went to the spirit world. As this lady comes forward, I know that you would have been very, very close to her before she passed. I feel that you helped to nurse her and kept trying to be with her before she passed over, washing her face, stroking her hair, all of these things before she went to the spirits. No matter how old this lady was, she still had life left in her and the desire to live and be strong in this world. This woman was a toughie in life, very emotionally strong. She tried to impart all the love she had for you before she went over. You were with this lady when she passed over? She's saying, "She was with me when I died." Were you?'

'Yes, I was,' Crystal replied, crying.

'There were three people with her when she died? She's saying that as her spirit left her body she was aware of the three people standing vigil over her. She made some silly comment about how dreadful she looked before she went over, but now she looks gorgeous. She became very gaunt in her face before she passed and she doesn't want you to remember her like that. She wants you to remember her fit and well. She was a very funny lady, who was always laughing and joking. She thinks you look like her. Her face is your face in the spirit world. You've been looking at her photograph just recently; holding her photograph in the last couple of days. Did you do that?'

Both Crystal and Catherine were crying now, but both nodded their heads.

'Yesterday,' Catherine added, 'we put my nanny to rest. She passed away around Christmas and we have just scattered her ashes in the ocean.'

'Did she lend some money to you?' I asked Crystal. 'Did she give you two thousand seven hundred dollars?'

'I am trying to think,' Crystal replied, doubtfully.

'Was it left to you? Willed to you? I'm so clear on the amount of money. Please remember two thousand seven hundred dollars. I think it will make sense, if not now, very shortly.'

'Now that I'm thinking about it,' Crystal suddenly interrupted, 'I know she owed two thousand seven hundred dollars on a credit card that we received when we issued the death certificate. I don't know if you've been picking up on that, but I certainly got the bill!'

Later, Catherine said to camera: 'I feel that my nanny led

Tony to us, so that we could have closure. We feel everything is now OK. I've watched those "afterlife" shows on TV and thought, "Oh my God, it would be so weird if that happened to me." Now it has happened, and I want to say thanks for letting it happen!'

All in all, making the special in San Francisco was a very *special* occasion.

People often approach me at public demonstrations and ask me if I ever get spooked by my work.

'No,' I reply, 'I don't get afraid, but my heart certainly races sometimes! And there are occasions when I think, "Oh hell! What's this? Am I about to pick up on something really traumatic?." Even when I do, though, I know that the experience will pass. It is not mine, it does not belong to me, and I do not need to hold on to it.'

This is absolutely true. As a medium, I simply need to remember that I am only the vessel for the relaying of information. Spooky experiences are also comparatively rare, and what I see on such occasions is probably no worse than what I sometimes catch a glimpse of on television. The vision is there; I do not want to look at it, but I do, then it is gone.

Sometimes I do experience a residual sense of emotion, which can be unpleasant for a time, but this is part of a medium's work, part of what we do. We have to learn how to detach ourselves emotionally very early on because we cannot afford to dwell too long on such things. If we do, we will 'crash', and not be in a fit state for the next demonstration or reading.

When the time came for me to film another television programme, this turned out to be an extravaganza entitled *The 3 Mediums Live at the Hammersmith Apollo*. In this show I was co-starring with two other mediums, Colin Fry and Derek Acorah. I am sure many people believe that Colin, Derek and I are great rivals, but this is not the case. The three of us have great respect for each other, and when we work together there is always a great atmosphere of support and encouragement.

I was not, I must confess, at my best at the start of the day on which the show was due to be filmed. When the chauffeur arrived to take me to the theatre, I had only had a few hours to catch up on sleep after flying back from San Franciso. I was so excited, though, that the adrenalin soon kicked in. This was the biggest psychic event I had ever been involved in, and when I got out of the limousine, there was a red carpet that led all the way from where the chauffeur had pulled over to the entrance of the theatre. As I greeted waiting fans on both sides of the roped-off area, I felt like a film star on BAFTA night! It proved to be a thrilling evening. There were over 3,000 people in the audience and I *loved* working with Colin and Derek.

The last reading I gave concerned a man in the spirit world whose body had been put into the boot of a car. Drawn to one particular area of the Apollo's massive auditorium, I stood a moment, my head on one side, listening, then said, 'I have a young man here, a troubled spirit, whose voice is not very clear, but he's saying something like three people who wanted to harm him bundled him into the boot of a car, and he died in there . . .'

A very nervous young girl connected with this and put up her hand. When Kerry was given the microphone, she was visibly trembling from head to toe, but she confirmed that a young man, who she knew very well, had died in the boot of a car.

'This fellow, who swears a lot,' I said, 'is saying that you are absolutely stunning. He's also saying something about when you were eleven years of age, or something that happened on the eleventh? He keeps on about this. He's also referring to something about the market, either nicking stuff or selling nicked stuff. I don't know whether you remember this particularly, but he's talking about some little yellow fluffy things that could be chicks; either he bought too many and didn't sell them, or there were a lot left over. Do you remember anything about this?'

'Yes,' Kerry replied at once. 'They were little yellow chicks and he couldn't get rid of them.'

Seconds later, I felt as if my arm had been broken and Kerry confirmed that he had broken his arm about a year before he died.

The next moment I saw the vision of a dog in my mind's eye.

'I've now got a dog here,' I said. 'A white Staffordshire Bull Terrier that was involved in dog fights. Did this man's dog have one black eye?'

'Yes – yes he did,' Kerry confirmed. 'And yes, the dog was used in dog fighting.'

Just as I was about to move on, I had another vision and, this time, I felt the sight go from my right eye.

'I now have a spirit here who is blind in one eye,' I said. 'It is my right eye that has just gone.'

'It's my sister,' Kerry cried out. 'She had a stroke and was left blind in her right eye.'

'Who is Denise?' I asked.

'It's her middle name,' Kerry gasped.

'She's saying she wanted someone to do her hair, but they didn't. Why didn't they?'

'When my sister was dying, we didn't do her hair.'

'Is it true that there were seven people at her bedside when she died?'

'Yes – we were all there.'

'She put her ring on your finger before she died?'

'Yes,' Kerry sobbed. 'I'm wearing it now.'

'She's sending you all her love, and saying something about a birthday. What does that mean?'

'It's my sister's birthday next month.'

'No, that doesn't feel right. She's saying something like today, tomorrow, within this little bit of now?'

'Oh my God! I've just remembered,' Kerry exclaimed, 'it's her daughter's birthday this Thursday.'

'She's saying "Happy Birthday".'

When Kerry was interviewed for the programme after the show, she told the camera crew that when her sister came through, that was the 'be-and-end-all of everything' for her. She had *so* needed to hear from her sister, and when her sister talked about the ring she had slipped on her finger, it was such a good experience. 'I would come again *any* time,' she added.

I was so pleased with that link because I think it is wonderful that the spirit people remember ordinary, everyday things like our birthdays and anniversaries. What better confirmation could there be that life – and love – endures and goes on.

One day when I was working at the Spiritualist Association of Great Britain (SAGB) in London, a very spooky message came through.

The Association puts on a big day there a couple of times a year, and I was doing a demonstration when I heard myself saying, 'There's a man here who is a very difficult character – a right villain, a hard nut, a crook, a nasty piece of work.'

A young woman, who thought she recognised this description, put up her hand and, when I added some more telling details, she nodded her head fervently and said, 'Oh yes, *absolutely*, that's him.'

'Well,' I replied, 'however villainous he was in life, darling, he is now in the spirit world and has met his mum, whose name, he tells me, is Vera.'

'Oh my God,' she exclaimed. 'I can't believe it. His mum's name was Vera.'

'He has just said that although he was an absolute bugger in life, his mother is now looking after him and has sorted him out.'

Just as I finished saying this, I had a truly horrific vision, which took my breath away and made me gasp. There he was lowering a man feet first into an industrial machine that was used for mincing meat. This was obviously a very scary, unpleasant piece of information to pass on at a public demonstration, but I knew it had to be offered up and I gave the information as delicately as I could.

Having described what I had just seen to the young lady, I added gently, 'Do you know anything about this?'

'*Absolutely*,' she said, her expression registering total astonishment that I could receive such accurate information from the spirit world. 'He was my boss, the publican of a pub that was frequented by villains and crooks. I managed the pub for him and the murder you've mentioned happened just before my time there. But I heard the story from several of the regulars.'

I guess we could be forgiven for thinking that such a person would come through from the spirit world with a completely different kind of 'feel' to other people, but no. He came through as a normal kind of guy, a person you would pass in the street without a backward glance. I knew, though, that even if he had got away with murder when he was alive, he would not escape the consequences of the horrors he had committed. In one way or another, the karma that would have resulted from his good and bad deeds would have to be worked through. He might, for example, be reborn into a situation where he was with people who behaved just as he did in his previous life. If, however, he had gone to the spirit world bowed down by a powerful sense of remorse and an ardent wish to make amends, who knows what his next embodiment might achieve.

In 2003, when I was preparing to do a demonstration with Colin Fry at the Apollo Theatre, Manchester, I had another very spooky experience – a rather physical one this time! Shortly before the show, I was washing my hair, as is my habit, in the bath. As I dunked my head in and out of the water to rinse off the shampoo, I suddenly had the awful sensation that I was drowning. I knew it was not me who was about to take my last breath, but the spirit of a middle-aged woman who had engaged my mind at that moment to show me how she had passed from this world.

As the drowning sensation passed, I lay back in the bath and said a prayer for her. I then added that I hoped she had not suffered too much and sent her on her way. I had a sense, however, that this was not the last time she would come to me.

Stepping out on to the stage of a large theatre is always a big moment, and rather than doing a double act when I am working with another medium, I prefer to have my own time to work and let the other person have their own time. I do not find chopping and changing beneficial. I like to create my own atmosphere. Learning how to work an audience is a very important part of demonstration work. If we allow the audience to become too passive or too hyper, too anything, then the energy is not good. No one can really teach this skill, though, it can only be learned from experience. A little two-way enthusiasm between the medium and the audience certainly helps, and if the first message is emotional, followed by another that is quite humorous, that also helps. I try to inject as much humour as possible into my demonstrations because that really livens the atmosphere.

To concentrate and be able to sense any spirits present, I

need to be calm. I often experience them as silhouettes or feel them walking or running around the centre or the back of the stage. The more tuned in I am, the more I can see. Often I can even see the colour of their eyes and hair.

That night at the Apollo, which seats about 2,000 people, Colin introduced me. 'Ladies and gentlemen, will you please welcome my good friend Tony Stockwell.' As soon as the clapping died down, I settled into my work and started the readings. The first spirit I was aware of was somebody I recognised. It was the lady I had encountered about an hour before in the bath.

'I have a middle-aged woman here,' I announced, 'a lady who drowned in a bath. Does anybody present recognise this person?'

A woman put up her hand and a microphone was handed to her.

I then went on to say that the woman was telling me that she had been drinking very heavily and was drunk and very depressed on the night she died, and that she had not meant to kill herself. It was all a terrible mistake.

'I fell asleep in the water,' she kept telling me, 'and I was *so* drunk, I just drowned.'

'She wants to thank you, darling,' I said to the woman in the audience, 'for sticking up for her. Apparently you have always said she would not have killed herself; that she only died because she fell asleep. She has now come through simply because she wants everybody to know that what you have always said is right. She did *not* kill herself.'

It was a good message with which to begin the evening, and I was feeling very upbeat and happy. The next message, however, was of a totally different order – *chilling* – and contained the kind of information that it is always difficult to give out during a public demonstration.

'Ladies and gentlemen,' I said tentatively, 'I have another lady here, a lady who I sense was battered to death. I am also getting a very strong feeling that she was battered to death by a man who was stalking her.'

A young girl in the audience gasped and put up her hand.

'My aunt,' she said tearfully, 'was battered to death by a man who wanted to have a relationship with her. When she refused, he started to stalk her and, one night, he attacked her in the street and beat her up. She managed to get away from him and run to her house, but he caught up with her and continued to beat her so badly he killed her.'

'Darling,' I said, 'she keeps on repeating, "send my love to Linda". Does that mean anything to you?'

'Linda's my mum,' she replied. 'Her sister.'

The spirit's voice was fading, but I was just able to hear her say, 'Tell Linda I'm OK now – I *really* am OK.'

Those were two very disturbing messages to receive that night, but they were also wonderfully powerful connections for those concerned.

People often ask me if mediums can cut off the spirit world if they want to, and the answer is, yes, of course. Most mediums are used to working between two worlds, but they can free themselves from the spirit world if they wish. This is done by controlling the mind and simply saying, 'I don't want to speak to you right now, thank you,' and turning this attention to something else. A spirit might give us another nudge and try again, but we do not have to respond. I have never encountered one who has taken over my life or got on my nerves.

All mediums have to discover for themselves when it is right to speak and when it is better to say nothing. If we do not, both our minds and sensitivity will be adversely affected. The best mediums maintain a healthy balance between this world and the spirit world, and home and family life and the necessity to achieve an income. If there is too much stress or an excess of rubbish in our lives, it can be very difficult to function as a medium because all our energies are engaged in material things.

When we are clear-headed, some extraordinary pieces of information can come through from the spirit world, but most of it is not at all grisly. On the contrary, most of it is very reassuring for the people concerned.

Recently, when I was doing a demonstration at the College of Psychic Studies, there was a queue for seats that went all the way down the stairs. We can only fit a hundred or so people in the room there, and this was already packed before I arrived. They were such a lovely, warm, energetic crowd that my first contact was very clear.

In my mind, I saw a man in his mid-thirties, who was very handsome, muscular and tanned, with dimples in his cheeks, wearing a blue T-shirt.

'Hiya, mate,' he said as he looked at me.

I was then shown that his death had involved a lorry. I gave out this information. To begin with, no one put up their hand. Then a lady, who was probably in her early sixties, raised her hand.

'Darling,' I said, 'do you know who this is?'

'Yes, I think I do,' she said.

'This man,' I added, having listened to the inner voice again, 'really loves you, and he keeps on saying that he was sorry to leave the three of you behind.'

'That's right,' she replied. 'Me and the two children.'

I could tell from her expression that it was proving to be a wonderful, much-needed message for her, and I said to him, 'Come on, mate, make sure she really knows that it's you.' Then, having listened, I said to her, 'He's now talking about Australia.'

At this she cried out, 'Oh my God, that's right. It really *is* him.'

'He's speaking to me with an Australian accent.'

'Yes, he would! He was Australian.'

It then transpired that he was her husband and that he had died some years previously.

'He's making a big thing now about the two lorries, darling,' I added.

'That's right. There were two lorries involved in the accident in which he died.'

The vision of him in my mind was so clear, so vibrant, that I knew exactly what he was feeling and saying. Although she was now in her sixties, he was looking at this woman as if she was in her twenties and he was absolutely adoring her.

'He's telling me that he will always love you,' I said.

'Please tell him I will always love him,' she sobbed.

Turning back to him, I said, 'Go on, tell her something *really* special,' and, in answer, he showed me a vision of a big tattoo on her back.

'Darling,' I said to her, 'he has just asked me to remind you of the tattoo, the large tattoo on your back?'

With that, she pulled up the top she was wearing and there, on her back, was a large tattoo of a lotus.

Towards the end of that day's demonstration I heard the name 'Diana' whispered in my ear.

'I have a lady here whose name is Diana,' I said to the group.

A lady put up her hand and I confirmed that the name I was hearing was definitely Diana, *not* Diane. 'That would be right,' she said.

Then I went on to describe a young woman with immaculate blonde hair who was beautifully dressed in a salmon-pink suit. Her voice was very posh and she was in her mid-thirties when she passed over. I had a strong sense of this woman standing by my side and, even while I was passing on various bits of information, I was beginning to think that her voice sounded exactly like Princess Diana's.

'She wants to thank you for all that you did for her,' I informed the lady in the audience, 'and also for all the thoughts and the love that you have sent to her since she passed over. You have helped to bring her closure. She is also talking about newspapers and saying that you must continue to be careful of the media. She knows you have been approached recently to tell your side of the story, but she really wants you to be very wary of doing so.'

'This has to be, Princess Diana,' I thought, but I did not mention this to the audience. That, I knew, would be an intrusion.

At the end of the demonstration, the lady came up to me and thanked me for the message. 'I don't know if you realised,' she whispered, 'but that was Princess Diana.'

'I did,' I replied, 'because the connection was so clear and the voice was unmistakeable.'

The lady did not tell me what her connection was with Princess Diana, but I sensed they were close to each other.

I am sure a number of people in the audience also realised who the spirit was, and I was not surprised when a number of them came up to me afterwards and said, 'That was Princess Diana, wasn't it?'

There are times when an enigmatic Mona Lisa smile is very useful in our work. That was one of them!

8

Prepared for Anything

Momentous moments and extraordinary events are pretty common in paranormal work, but some, however much time elapses, remain etched on our minds forever. One particularly haunting event occurred for me in 2001, a period when I had a number of clients in the Belgrave Square area of London. During this time, I struck up a friendship with a lady called Lesley who was a friend of a lady called Astrid, the personal assistant of the singer/actress, Cher. One night Lesley mentioned that she and Astrid were looking after the place where Cher stayed when she visited London. The singer had taken out a long-term lease on this residence so that she could use it as her UK home.

'Whenever Astrid or I are alone there,' Lesley added, 'we are absolutely convinced that it's haunted, and that there are some really bizarre paranormal things going on under its roof. Could you come round when we're there one night and see if you can sense anything strange about the place.'

Intrigued, I arranged to go there one evening with Carol Bohmer, a medium friend.

En route, I realised I hadn't asked Astrid what type of building we were visiting and, as a result, I hadn't a clue whether we were going to a flat, a house, an old or a modern building. When we arrived in the locality, however, I decided to park the car and walk the short distance to the address we had been given, so we could get a 'feel' of the area.

'It's very strange,' Carol said as we wandered down the

street, 'but although I know we are going to Cher's home, I keep getting an image flitting through my mind of Paula Yates – Bob Geldofs ex-wife – who passed over about a year ago.'

'That *is* strange,' I agreed.

'What about you?' Carol asked as we continued on our way. 'Have you picked up anything yet?'

'Yes, and it's also weird,' I replied. 'I keep getting a vision of Tutankhamen.'

'Tutankhamen!' Carol snorted. 'Well, that's us sorted for the night then. It doesn't sound as if it's going to be a very promising visit, does it?'

Minutes later, although we knew we were in the right street, we were having great difficulty in locating the number we had been given. Then, suddenly, we found ourselves outside a tall, modern office block. Initially we were puzzled – this didn't seem right at all – but then we saw that between this building and the next there was a tiny, dark, mysterious-looking alleyway, and at the end of this was a gate which, unbelievably, led to a miniature castle, complete with slit-eyed windows and decorative turrets sporting gargoyles. It was a bizarre building to find sandwiched between two modern office blocks, and it looked as if it had fallen out of the sky from another century or had been built as a set for a film.

Barely recovered from our shock, we knocked on its grey oak door and were greeted by Lesley and Astrid.

Stepping inside was like being fast-tracked back in time. Everything in the six-bedroomed, stone-built and wood-panelled castle was antique, most of it original to the place. And although the lounge area had a huge, cavernous open fire, which gave off a welcoming glow, the overall atmosphere of the place was dark, foreboding and rather chilly. Both Carol and I felt at once that the castle was seriously haunted, and as we opened our senses to our surroundings, we became more and more aware that the place was 'alive', positively humming with spirits from a former age. The sense that we had walked into a sinister time-warp was very real for both of us.

After we had sat silently, eyes closed, in the lounge for a few minutes, Lesley and Astrid asked us if we had seen or felt anything.

'Monks – lots of monks,' Carol replied at once.

'Serving maids,' I added. 'And although this property is now surrounded by modern office blocks, all I could see was acres of meadows, fringed by bulrushes, teasels and a large lake.'

I was then made aware that there was a definite religious link with the place; I sensed there had once been a monastery on the spot, that monks had lived and passed through the area, and that medieval serving girls had traipsed to and fro from a nearby inn.

When we began to walk around the castle, the doors creaked and gave out eerie groans, and all the lights flickered as if the place were lit by oil lamps or candles. The furniture was made from heavy, dark wood, and there were carvings of gargoyles on the wooden banisters and doors. The whole place had a totally surreal feel about it.

At one point, when I found myself alone in a bedroom, I felt the spirit of a man step inside my body and walk right through me. I must have gasped because Carol rushed into the room and, moments later, said that she could see four monks performing what looked like a rather 'iffy' ritual.

Carol and I were so in tune with each other that night that we were both able to sense and see the same group of monks walking to and fro in the wood-panelled room. After a moment or two, having picked up on something else, I called out to Lesley and Astrid and asked if there was anything beyond the room we were standing in. Lesley pointed to a door that was secreted in the panelling and when I opened this

I discovered it led to a narrow, stone, spiral staircase that went up to the roof.

Once we had climbed up there and recovered from nearly being blown off by a gale-force wind, Carol and I were both drawn to look over the parapet. It was a dark, moonless night, but there below us we could see a vision of the twisted body of a man. Moments later, without saying a word to each other, we both sensed that he had been thrown to his death from the spot where we were now standing – and for a minute or two, the hairs stood up on the back of my neck. We also sensed, although there was no way we could prove it, that at one time the place where the castle now stood had been attached to another building, and that there had been a maze of mysterious underground tunnels leading to and from them.

A little later, as we walked into a room which contained a large four-poster bed, it was Carol's turn to gasp. Turning to me, she exclaimed, 'Oh my God, Tony! I can see Paula Yates lying on that bed.'

As we moved into the room's en suite bathroom, we were joined by Lesley and Astrid.

'What's happening? What are you feeling?' they asked.

'I don't know why,' Carol replied, 'but I keep feeling the presence of Paula Yates in this bedroom and bathroom. I've already seen her lying on the bed and now I can feel her lying on the floor in here.'

Having exchanged knowing glances, Lesley and Astrid then said, 'Well, that's amazing because we happen to know that Paula Yates used to stay here. And where we are now standing was her bedroom, and on one occasion she was found collapsed in this bathroom.'

Carol was very pleased: 'That's the Paula Yates link resolved,' she said smugly, 'but what about your Tutankhamen link, Tony?'

Turning to Lesley and Astrid, I said, 'Are there any areas we haven't yet seen?'

'Only the courtyard,' Lesley replied.

'Lead on,' I answered.

To be honest, I was not really expecting anything, but, as we stepped outside, I stopped dead in my tracks and my mouth dropped open. I could hardly believe my eyes. There in the middle of the shadowy, cobbled courtyard was a life-size statue of Tutankhamen.

'*Yes*' I hooted, surely startling any ghosts that were around. 'He's here, Carol. *He's here*!'

Altogether, it was an extraordinary evening, one that has lived on in my memory, but the most wonderful thing about the whole experience was that it showed how two mediums could work together in total unity.

To this day, I have no way of knowing whether Cher is aware that the place she leased for her London visits is alive, humming with spirit energy, or whether she was ever told that Lesley and Astrid invited me to visit it. But I am not concerned. Cher has the look of a person who can cope with most things in this life – and in the afterlife!

A momentous reading that stands out in my mind is one that I did for a lady called Kim. In her early forties, she was my first client of the day and preceded her sister who had booked the next appointment. Having journeyed from Birmingham, she was forty minutes late for her one-hour appointment, and when she arrived she was obviously stressed, out of breath and feeling very emotional.

'I'm *so* sorry I'm late,' she gasped. 'And thank you *so* much for seeing me. I'm pinning all my hopes on this experience.'

Such a statement puts a lot of pressure on a medium and I was particularly keen for the spirits to do well for her that day.

The first to come through was her mother, who said that she had a man alongside her who had only recently passed over into the spirit world. When I mentioned this to Kim, and added that I could feel a guy in his forties standing alongside me, she became very tearful.

'My husband,' she said, 'died a year ago.'

I then heard the man telling me that he and Kim had had three children.

'Tell me their names,' I pleaded, knowing that such evidence would convince Kim that it really was he who was present.

The next moment, I caught the name Louise, and I asked her if that was the name of one of their children.

'No,' came the answer.

In my mind, I was silently grumbling at the spirit people, asking where, then, had this particular name come from? Then I heard him telling me that it was one of their children's middle names, and this time I heard the name Emma-Louise resounding in my mind.

'Does the name Emma-Louise mean anything to you?' I asked Kim.

'It's my daughter's name,' she gasped.

I passed on that her husband was sending his love to Emma-Louise. Then I turned my attention to getting the names of their two sons. The name Mark entered my mind, but again this proved to be a middle name. Why middle names were in so much evidence that day, I will never know! Then the letter 'J' lit up in my mind and I felt sure that this stood for James.

'Does the name James-Mark mean anything to you?' I asked Kim.

'That's the name of our eldest son,' she replied, amazed.

So far so good, but sadly, hard as I tried, I could not get the name of the third child. Instead of giving up at once, though, I made a big thing about this to the spirit, saying that surely he did not want to miss out this child, who he had obviously loved as much as the other two. For some unknown reason I still could not make the connection. I was, though, able to tell Kim how and when her husband died, and what a loving, honest, humble man he had been, and I was also able to give her a personal message from him.

All in all, Kim was greatly touched by the reading, and when I went to reception I found her in floods of happy tears, being comforted by her sister and her daughter.

That reading, which had contained so much spot-on information, including the names of two of their children, had cast aside any doubts she might have had that we were in touch with the spirits of her loved ones, and it had contained truly momentous moments for both of us.

For me personally, it was a reminder of what an extraordinary thing it is for mediums like myself to be able to offer people the right names from the hundreds of thousands of names that exist, and what a major impact this ability can have on a person's belief in the afterlife. As a medium I know that the spirit world is encircling us all of the time, and that, whether others appreciate it or not, we are constantly interacting with it. But I have never become blasé and it is still wonderful for me when, thanks to a reading, other people are helped to realise that true love has no boundaries and continues to exist beyond the grave.

There was another momentous moment in store for me when a friend called Barb (Barbara) phoned me one day and said that her sister, Pam, had seen me on TV and was desperate for a reading. Pam was coming down from Leicester at the weekend, and would I *please* read for her.

The lady, one of Barb's older sisters in her fifties, proved to be a very pleasant woman, and when I began the reading, while Barb sat silently on a settee in the corner of the room, I was astonished by the amount of information that was coming through for her. The first spirit I picked up on was that of a tall, thin man who had been in the spirit world for quite some time.

'This tall, thin man thinks the world of you,' I began, 'and he is making me feel that you have suffered from chronic pain in your back. He is rubbing your back and trying to bring some healing to it – and to your neck. This man has been overlooking you from the spirit world for the past year, because it has been a very difficult time for you and he wants you to know that he is always there to guide you. He is also referring to a ring that he bought you. He wants you to look after this ring and keep it close to you. He wants to thank you for being with him when he passed, when his spirit was leaving his body. He didn't want to die and he was scared of dying. You were on his right side the last time you were with him, and although he could not respond, he could feel you touching his face. Do you understand?'

'The tall, thin man was my father,' Pam said. 'He died thirty years ago. Nobody knows this, but I have kept his ring all these years. It is very comforting to know that he has been looking after me this past year.'

'The other man who is present,' I said, 'is much younger than the tall, thin man, and his build is stocky. Before he passed he was feeling very agitated, and he wants to say sorry for some of the things that he said to you. He is making me feel that you spoiled him in a very nice way, that you doted on him.'

'He was my son,' Pam said, beginning to weep.

'I feel that he knew he was ill before he passed, but he kept dismissing it from his mind. His attitude was if we don't talk about it, we won't have to deal with it. I think he neglected his health and would not be told what to do by the doctors. He's referring to being out of sorts, and not at all like himself for the last three days of his life. Before he passed, although he had been a very strong young man, he went down hill rapidly. He had terrible breathing problems and was on an oxygen mask. He is telling me that you kept trying to make sure that he was comfortable, and kept fiddling with the straps around his ears. He wasn't bothered by this, but he was aware of what you were doing. You also kept dabbing water on his lips?'

'Yes.' Pam's responses were now so muffled by her tears that I could hardly hear her. 'He wasn't allowed to drink water, so I kept his lips moist with a little sponge on a stick.'

'Do you also remember drying a tear as it trickled from his eye down his cheek?'

'Yes. When he was very weak, near the end, I held one of his hands and his sister held the other. We told him how much we loved him and, when a tear rolled down his cheek, I wiped it and other tears from his eyes.'

'You've kept a piece of jewellery that belonged to him. You are wearing his chain?'

'Yes, it's actually a bracelet and I'm wearing it now.'

'His sister has a son. There's a very close feeling between him and this boy. It really is very strong. They have the same name – the same *middle* name?'

'Yes. He adored his nephew, and the boy, my grandson, adored him. And yes, they do both have the same middle name, and to look into my grandson's eyes is like looking into the eyes of my son.'

'There's a watch that he bought, a watch that he only wore on special occasions. And do you still have this watch?'

'Yes.'

'He wants it to be given to his nephew – your grandson – for his eighteenth birthday.'

'I had planned to give the watch to him when he reached eighteen,' Pam gasped.

'I know roses are very popular,' I added, 'but your son is wanting to bring red roses to you – really black-red roses.'

'Yes – yes,' Pam sobbed.

'I'm sensing that this is because you bought him red roses after he died, and he now wants to return these roses with his love.'

'He *loved* roses,' Pam replied. 'He even incorporated the word "rose" in his e-mail address. I had a cushion of roses made for his funeral and I tried, without success, to get a black rose to plant in the memorial garden. Now, in the garden of my house, I have about forty rose bushes, including some black ones. This Christmas Eve, when I went out into the garden, I found that two of the roses, "Black Velvet" and "Remember Me", were in bloom. It was the first time I have ever had roses in flower at that time of year.'

'He now wants to talk to me about you cutting his hair. He's remembering you made the best of a bad job?'

'Yes, I cut his hair when he was very poorly.'

'Did your son like cars? Did he ever want an Aston Martin?'

'Yes!' Pam was amazed. 'Enver, my son, worked in car electronics and cars were his life. Every day when we had to go to the hospital for his radiotherapy we passed a garage that had an Aston Martin in the showroom. Every day he would say, "There's my car in there," and, to cheer him up, I would reply, "One day – *one day*".'

'He wants me to tell you that he has an Aston Martin in the spirit world.' I paused a moment, listening. 'Your father is now here again, sending you love and telling me that you and your sister, Barb, had *different* fathers. Was your father a difficult man when he was alive?'

'Yes.'

'He's apologising for having made your mother's life diffi-cult, and is telling me that he is now a reformed character – altogether a brighter, lighter man.' I paused again as my mind was led off on a different track. 'To your knowledge, did the mother of your grandson ever lose a baby?'

'Yes,' Pam sobbed. 'My daughter had a miscarriage at the time Enver, my son, was very ill.'

'It was a girl baby she lost. Did you know that?'

'No, we didn't know the sex of the child.'

'You must ask your daughter whether she would have called the baby Katie if she had lived, because that is what she has been called in the spirit world.'

I paused, listening again.

'Your son is now saying that he has the baby with him in the spirit world, and that he will look after her. He is also saying that he will look after your grandson in our world.'

I paused again.

'Your son is sorry for ruining Christmas. Did he die around about that time?'

'Yes, just after.'

'He's showing me the time that he died on the watch. It seems to me that he died at 1.25 pm, or is it 4.05 pm? It's strange as I am being shown both times.'

'You are spot on,' Pam sobbed, amazed. 'After the doctors told me that there was no hope for him, the life-support machine was switched off at 1.25 pm and he died at 4.05.'

'He's now drawing me to a ring that you are wearing on your finger today that is not your own. Has it belonged to anyone else?'

'I don't know. I found it in my daughter's garage.'

'I sense that this ring was brought to you by the spirit people. There is,' I added as I concluded the reading, 'so much love coming from him to you, and that love will *never* die; love *cannot* die. You must also remember that your son can come to you whenever he wants to – and I believe that you will become very receptive to his presence.'

Later, Pam told Barb and everybody else that this reading was so important for her, it had actually saved her sanity and her life.

Her son, Enver, I learned, was a very handsome guy who, having been ill for a very long time, died from cancer when he was just twenty years old. His spirit came so close to us that day, and the connection was so clear, I was able to tell Pam many deeply personal things that he wanted her to hear. Although she wept throughout the reading, the messages were very healing.

Pam also appreciated the significance of the gold ring that was mentioned. The ring, which she found in a box in her daughter's garage and which had seemingly come from no-where, turned out to be of a Turkish design, and her son had been half-Turkish. She also confirmed that although Barb had said that the two of them were sisters, they were in fact *half*-sisters who, after many attempts, had only managed to trace each other a few months before the reading.

Since the reading, Pam has sent me a tapestry of my face. Having transferred a photographic image of me on to the canvas, she spent many months lovingly stitching it in needle-point. It is a work of art – and I was very touched by her gift.

I found myself in for yet another lovely surprise when an Irish lady in her sixties named Margaret came to see me recently in Wickford. As soon as she entered the room, she reminded me that she had first come to see me about a year ago, but at that time I had drawn a complete blank and had been unable to read for her.

'Come back on another occasion,' I had suggested.

Margaret had remembered my advice, had made another booking, and this time proved to be very different from the first.

'Your father is in the spirit world,' I began.

'Yes.'

'Would you understand why your father keeps saying sorry?'

'Yes, I think I would.'

'Darling,' I replied, 'you didn't know your father well?'

'That's right,' she answered.

I was aware that something was happening to my mind that does not often occur. It felt huge, as if it contained universes, and was opening up to everything.

'Your mother was young, your father was young, and their love was forbidden,' I said.

'Absolutely,' she replied.

'They came from completely different classes.'

'Yes, my mother was from a very poor background and my father from a very rich one.'

'Your father was a very kind, loving man who never wanted to give your mother up. But he was put under tremendous pressure and, when your mother became pregnant with you, his parents paid for his name *not* to be included on your birth certificate.'

'Oh my God!' she cried out. 'It really *is* him. I was told when I was an adult that his parents had paid my grandparents a hundred pounds not to include his name on the birth certificate, and that they had then forced my parents to part company.'

'I'm not sure I quite understand this,' I added, 'but he keeps saying that you should send his love to your mum.'

'Yes. My mother is still alive.'

'But darling,' I added, 'I'm also picking up that you have a mother in the spirit world.'

Margaret looked at me for a moment, then said, 'When I was born, my mother gave me to my grandmother who then brought me up – and I always thought my gran was my mother. I grew up in Ireland with my grandparents, but when I was seventeen I left and came to England and eventually got married here. My grandmother died shortly after this. Meanwhile, my biological mother, who I knew as "auntie" had also married, but she only told her other children that I existed when I was in my forties.'

Margaret then went on to tell me that when she went back to Ireland, her mother told her everything. After that, Margaret made contact with her father, who was living in Australia, and met him on four occasions before he died. During these meetings, he always impressed on her that he had never wanted to give her mother up, but had been forced to go along with his parents' wishes.

Margaret was so thrilled that I was able to give her such a comprehensive reading on the second attempt. She found the fact that her father was still sorry, even in the spirit world, very emotional. And she could hardly believe that I had been able to unravel such a complicated family history. It was real evidence for her that there was life after death.

I have no idea why I could not read for Margaret the first time. That will have to remain one of those mysteries!

As a psychic medium, I have learned over the years that I need to be prepared for anything. Although nine times out of ten the communications that come through from the spirit world are very pleasant, this is not always the case. Some are quite troubling and disturbing. Messages from people who have committed suicide can be difficult enough to pass on

sometimes, but messages from spirits who have been murdered are even more difficult and need to be handled with
great sensitivity and care. When I first began work as a
medium, I was tempted to resist giving out painful or unpleasant information to loved ones, but I now know that such
messages are given for a purpose and it would not be right for
me to act as censor and withhold the information that is given.
My role is not to rationalise or to doubt what I see or hear, but
to trust the spirits and pass on what they tell me. This was
confirmed yet again when I was working in a small town in
north Germany. While I was there I stayed with Christina
Hesse, a lovely lady and medium, who has been a medical
doctor all her working life.

One of the readings I was called upon to do was for a
mother and daughter who had left Russia many years ago to
emigrate to Germany. During the sitting, Christina acted as
my interpreter. It is very challenging working in this way. I
have to be very precise about the words I use because if I am
not, the message can get lost in translation, or a wrong
emphasis can set up a negative response. For example, if I
say, 'Your father tells me that he could be difficult at times',
this could be translated as: 'Your dad was a very difficult man
in life.' The implication is different and may result in: 'No –
that's not right. My dad was a *lovely* man.' I am always
mindful, then, that I must speak with great precision when
working abroad.

When I began reading for Alana and her daughter, I
immediately picked up that they had both been physically
and sexually abused by the woman's husband, and I was able
to describe his appearance and the kind of person he was.
Early on in the reading, both Alana and her daughter became
very distressed and were clutching at each other's hands while
sobbing and crying. It was an emotional experience for me,

too, and there were moments when I felt an overwhelming compassion for them. It was not easy for me to continue, but I sensed that this was a long overdue experience that could prove to be cleansing and healing for both of them.

At one moment I had a very clear vision in my mind's eye of a squalid little flat, fronted by a small balcony. Although it was freezing cold outside, with temperatures obviously below zero, there was a little dog, who was whimpering and very distressed, on the balcony. I described the setting and the two women confirmed that they had lived there. When I then described the dog, they broke down again and sat crying their hearts out.

'This dog died on the balcony,' I added.

'Yes,' Alana replied through her tears. 'Although it was the middle of the Russian winter, my husband terrorised us into doing nothing and he wouldn't let the dog back into the flat. The dog, which my daughter and I loved so dearly, froze to death on that balcony.'

'Your mother,' I then told Alana, 'was also a very difficult woman in life, but she is in the spirit world now and she is holding a baby in her arms – a little baby boy.'

'*No*,' Alana instantly blurted out, becoming very agitated. 'That's not true. I don't know any baby boy. *No*.'

It was one of those moments when I could have been forgiven for backing off, but that was not what the spirit required of me. The image I had seen was extremely vivid.

'The baby your mother is holding is her son – your brother,' I said, feeling compelled to continue, 'She is telling me that she has the baby, and that she is very sorry for what she did. She wants you to know that the baby has forgiven her and they are together again.'

'*No*,' Alana insisted again. 'This is not right. I do not know anything about a baby.'

But she could not keep up the pretence any longer. All of a sudden her face crumpled and her resistance broke. She sat there weeping as if her heart would break.

'Darling,' I said gently, having listened to the spirit again, 'your mother is telling me that she was responsible for the death of her child.'

'Yes . . .'

Having found just enough inner strength to confirm this, the floodgates opened again, then slowly, with Christina translating, it emerged that when Alana was a young woman living in Russia, she and her mother had been made destitute and had no money with which to buy food for her baby brother, who was crying day and night from hunger pains. Since then, although she had tried to blot out the agonising memory, she was still haunted by the events that had led up to her mother smothering the baby.

For her, the reading was a very painful, but very powerful experience, and the message of understanding and forgiveness that it contained was badly needed. By the end of the session, I felt quite sure that she could now continue to live out her life much less burdened by the terrible weight of pain and grief that she had carried throughout the intervening years.

The same was true for a young lady I read for during a demonstration in Gibraltar. I visit this country about four times a year to work in a club called The Black Cat. Because Gibraltar is a devout Catholic country and many Catholics – like many fundamentalist Christian groups – think that 'talking to the dead is evil', we invariably have a hardcore group of protestors who proclaim I am a devil and a devil worshipper.

One result of these strong feelings is that many of the people who come along to the demonstrations arrive with coats over their heads. They are afraid that if they are spotted by their priests or neighbours they will be harassed and told that they will 'go to hell for dabbling in such evil things'. Despite the prejudice, though, I have discovered that there is a huge need among Gibraltarians to learn about the paranormal and spirit communication. And, perhaps because the need is so great, I work really well there. Certainly the message I gave to the young English lady living there was one of the best and most prolonged that I have ever given.

'I have a young man here whose name is David,' I began.

'That's right,' she replied, shocked. 'He was a very dear friend of mine.'

'Please forgive me if I am wrong,' I continued, 'but I sense this man committed suicide because he couldn't cope with life and was very afraid of what others would think of him.'

'Yes,' the young woman replied, beginning to weep. 'He just couldn't come to terms with what he saw as his failings.'

All of a sudden, I felt the young man standing right alongside me, holding a little boy by the hand.

'He has a little boy, aged about six, standing next to him,' I said, 'and the child's name is Peter.'

At this, the young woman let out a cry like a wounded animal.

'What does this mean?' I asked, turning to her friend who had come with her.

'It's her son,' the woman answered, startled. 'He died when he was six years old.'

'I don't know for sure what happened to him,' I continued, 'but I'm now getting the sensation of something pulled very tight around my neck.'

Minutes later, when both women had recovered sufficiently to be able to speak, I was told that the little boy had been playing in his room and that during the boisterous game, the cord of his dressing-gown had got tangled around his neck and he had accidentally hung himself when he was climbing down from his bunk-bed.

'Your son is now with David,' I said, 'and David wants you to know that he is being a good father to Peter.'

'David was my best friend,' the woman sobbed. 'I know he would look after Peter.'

I thought that was that, but suddenly I had a vision of David and Peter accompanied by a young woman. This time, aware of an overpowering feeling of evil, I felt shaky, generally ill at ease, and rather reluctant to continue. The next moment, though, my awareness of the physical surroundings of the club completely disappeared, and I found myself entirely focused on the vision of the young woman walking down an English street. As I walked alongside her in my mind, I saw a little restaurant to one side of me, and I knew at once that something awful had happened there. The young woman, I realised a moment later, had been abducted from this place. Then, as clear as day, I was shown a chilling image.

'I have a young lady here now who is talking about Sherwood Forest,' I said tentatively to the woman. 'She is saying that her body was found in Sherwood Forest. Was this person a friend of yours?'

'Yes she was,' the woman gasped, and when she had managed to recover her wits yet again, she told me that a friend of hers had been abducted from outside a restaurant. Snatched from the street and bundled into a car, she had been found murdered in the forest.

'They caught the murderer because they found his coat?' I queried.

'Yes, he left his coat over her body.'

Having described the coat, I heard her friend in the spirit world call: 'He's coming out soon.'

'Yes,' the young woman confirmed. 'He's due for release in the next month or so.'

Then I got his name and this too was confirmed.

When I was giving this message I was standing by a stone column in the club, and all of a sudden I sensed an arc-shaped veil being lifted higher and higher. As it rose, the room in which the demonstration was taking place completely disappeared. In paranormal circles, people often talk about the veil that exists between our world and the next, but this was the only time I had ever seen it for myself, and, as I did so, one spirit face after another appeared. I felt as if I was in the spirit world communicating with the living.

Sometimes a reading can prove to be an embarrassment for the person concerned. I am now recalling an occasion when a mother and daughter came for a reading. The daughter, a very pleasant-looking, fun person, was aged about forty-five and her mum was in her seventies. As soon as I saw the daughter, I sensed that she had had a really bad marriage and that her ex-husband had been an aggressive, bullish man.

When I mentioned this, she replied, 'That's absolutely right. The marriage was *awful* and so was he.'

'You are in a relationship now?' I said.

'No,' she replied firmly, 'I am not.'

This answer did not accord with what I was picking up, but I carried on regardless and, turning to the mother, I said, 'I have your mum here, but I feel you also had another mum who was your auntie.'

'Yes, that's right,' she replied, astonished.

'And there was a time when you nursed both of these women, who were sisters in life, and you loved them both equally as your mother.'

'Yes,' she replied, impressed. 'I did.'

'Your auntie is telling me that she was a spinster who never had any children of her own.'

'Yes, I was like a daughter to her.'

'Darling,' I said, swivelling back to the daughter, 'you've told me you are not in a relationship, and I don't want to pry, but your auntie is telling me that you *are* in a relationship – a relationship that is very important to you.'

The expression on the daughter's face was not encouraging. She was looking at me as if to say, '*Please* don't say any more.'

At this point, having paused for a moment, I asked if I could have a few minutes alone with her. Once her mother had left the room, I sat listening to her auntie again and, as she was still very insistent that I should continue as before, I said to the girl, 'Your auntie keeps telling me that she never got married because she didn't feel comfortable around men, and that you are just like her. She is *very* pleased – and wants everybody else to be pleased – that you are now in a loving relationship with a woman. She is saying that you must not be ashamed, and that you need to find the courage to talk to your mother about your partner and to ask your mother to include this person in her life. You are a good person and a good daughter, and your mother, your auntie says, needs to accept you for who and what you are.'

The girl nodded her head a couple of times as I finished speaking, but no more was said and the reading came to an end.

After the session, I took the opportunity to speak to the woman who had organised the readings.

'What do you know about the young woman?' I asked.

'Oh, she's a *lovely* person,' she replied. Then, lowering her voice to a whisper, she added, 'She's gay, you know, and lives with a woman partner.'

'Yes,' I replied, smiling, 'that much I know!'

The reading might have been a bit of a shock for the daughter, but I sensed even before she left the room that it had been a *healing* session, and that a change for the good had come about. Mother and daughter seemed much closer to each other than when they had arrived. And, for me, this was yet further confirmation that the sprits really do know what they are doing!

Another occasion when this proved to be true was when I was doing a one-to-one reading in southern Spain. When the elderly lady who had booked the appointment arrived, I was surprised to see that she was dressed in black from head to toe and clutching rosary beads. She really was the living embodiment of a very religious-looking, older Catholic, and such people did not usually make appointments to see me. Mentally I groaned, thinking I was in for a very tough time.

'She's probably come to test me,' I thought. 'She will have a closed mind, will harden her heart against me, and I honestly don't know whether I will be able to work with her.'

I could not have been more wrong. This lady gave proof to the old adage that you should never judge a book by its cover!

As the reading began, I instantly saw, standing behind her, a young man.

'I have a young man here,' I said, 'who is telling me he is your son.'

'Yes,' she replied, 'he is the reason why I have come here today. I miss him terribly.'

'Your son has just said that he passed six months ago.'

'Yes, that's correct,' she replied, beginning to look tearful. 'It was in June. He passed just a few days before his birthday.'

'So far, so good,' I thought, relieved. But the next moment I was absolutely thrown. The vision I was now being shown was crystal clear, but it was the same young man dressed as a woman and wearing a glamorous, green, sequined dress. I began to panic. How could I tell this tear-stained elderly lady sitting in front of me, clutching her rosary, that I could see her son in the spirit world wearing a frock that would not have been out of place on the set of *Moulin Rouge!* After a short pause that seemed to go on forever, I could hold back no longer.

'Darling' I began very gently, 'I have absolutely no idea why your son is showing me this image of himself, but he is now wearing the most sparkly green dress I have ever seen.'

As I finished speaking, the lady fought back her tears and burst out laughing.

'That's *right*!' she exclaimed. 'He was a drag queen in life, and I helped him sew every single green sequin on that dress. It was his absolute favourite.'

As the reading continued, the man revealed that he had passed with AIDS, that most of his family and his church had rejected him, and that his mum had been the only one who was always there for him. She was one of his biggest fans, who had helped him to make his costumes and who had watched him perform whenever she could.

The mention of the dress was one of the most evidential pieces of information I could have given to the lady to prove that her son had not gone forever, that he was still part of her life and still exactly the same person in the spirit world that he had been in life. To think I had been reluctant to tell her what I had seen!

While I was putting the finishing touches to this book in 2004, I was working with my good friends Colin Fry and Lizzie Faulkner on another pilot for Hilary and Craig Goldman at IPM. Entitled *Psychic Detective*, the idea behind this new television series was for three clairvoyants – Colin, Lizzie and myself – to use our psychic skills to solve unsolved mysteries and murder cases. To assist us in this, we had a private detective working alongside us on the programme, and the plan was for us to give him any leads we picked up. He would then investigate these and let us know if what we had sensed was true.

Included in this pilot was a sequence in which we tried to identify the body of the unnamed person who was burned to death in the King's Cross fire in 1987. We soon learned that, despite painstaking detective work and a reconstruction of the man's face by computer imaging, the identity of the man had remained a mystery for seventeen years. Having died alongside thirty others in the fire, he was known only as Body 115 – the number the mortuary officials had given to his charred body.

To get the *Psychic Detective* pilot off the ground, we first went to Scotland to do a reading for one of two Scottish families who thought the unidentified man might be their missing dad. To help us, we also looked at photographs of the body, visited King's Cross station, where the tragedy was thought to have been set into motion by somebody dropping a still-burning cigarette butt on an escalator, and visited his graveside in a North London cemetery.

While we were at the graveside of the unknown man, all three of us experienced the weirdest feelings. Lizzie and I felt that we were being physically rocked to and fro, and at one point we felt that we were being spun around. I can't explain what was happening, but we were certainly in contact with a strange energy. It was almost as if the spirits in that place were watching the three of us and trying to encourage us to feel more so that we could establish the identity of Body 115.

When we went down the escalator into King's Cross station, we found ourselves drawn to the area where most of the people had lost their lives in the tragedy. Opening our minds, we travelled back in time and found ourselves experiencing some of the fear that had been present in that place at that time. It really was a terrible tragedy for all the people and the families concerned, and to be honest we could not wait to get out of there.

The format for the pilot, which was totally different from our usual run of work, stretched our psychic powers to the limit, and when we were making it, both Colin and I picked up some very disturbing things about the first Scottish family's missing dad. Independently of each other, we both felt sure that the unidentified body did *not* belong to their father. Then, using our combined psychic powers, we felt that their dad had ended his days as a down-and-out who was constantly on the move from one place to another.

Colin also picked up that, on one occasion, the man had gone searching for his daughter in a seaside town where there were cable cars. At this point it was revealed that his daughter had lived in Brighton at the time.

Lizzie and I also had a vision of the front door of a house, and when we both described it as green, the woman confirmed that they had once lived there.

There was obviously some useful synchronisation going on between Colin, Lizzie and I, and it was reassuring for us and the team to know that we were on the same wavelength.

During the investigation, I also began to sense that the family's missing father had been murdered, and I picked up that this had happened near water, possibly a canal. Independently of me, Colin also gleaned that the man had been murdered alongside a canal.

It is obviously very difficult to report to a family that you believe their father was beaten to death, but in the end I overcame my resistance and did just that. It is always best, I believe, to be completely honest – and the whole point of this particular television programme was to be a psychic detective and hopefully solve a mystery.

Having established that their father was *not* a victim of the King's Cross fire, Colin, Lizzie and I were then filmed conducting a séance in a darkened room. For this, we all did some trance work, and the spirits spoke through us. At this point in the séance, I decided to do some automatic writing.

'Who are you?' Colin called out.

As he did so, my pen began to move. When it stopped, we looked down at the sheet of paper and saw the name 'Alex' written there.

The conclusion that we came to was that the unidentified man was Alexander Fallon – a name that was included on a list of three possible names that we were given before we started work. After we finished filming that day, our report was handed to the police.

Several weeks later, on 22 January 2004, I was reading a copy of the *Daily Mirror* and, as I turned a page, I was in for a shock. There, to my astonishment, was a headline: '*The final victim*'. As I read on, my eyes widened. The police had finally identified the thirty-first victim of the King's Cross blaze as seventy-two-year-old Alexander Fallon.

A former salesman, the copy read, Alexander had left his home in Falkirk, Scotland, suffering from a broken heart after his wife had died from cancer in December 1974. At first he had kept in touch with his four daughters, but as the years passed and his own health apparently deteriorated, his calls became fewer and fewer, until they ceased altogether.

It was now thought, the newspaper feature continued, that he had spent the last year or so of his life living rough, sometimes begging at King's Cross station to supplement his benefits. One possible reason why it had taken so long for him to be identified was that the supposed age of the unidentified victim had been given as between forty to sixty, and Alexander Fallon was in his early seventies when he died.

It was one of his daughters, Mary Leisham, who finally contacted the British Transport Police.

'My three sisters and I often asked each other when we met or spoke, 'Have you heard from our father?', but it was only in 1997, when a cousin we met in church suggested he might have been a victim in the fire that we really started thinking.'

Then, in 2003, when Mary read about a memorial service that was being held for the fire's victims, she decided to go to the police to put her cousin's hunch to the test. Detectives then established that her father, Alexander Fallon, had claimed no more benefits after November 1987 and that there was no record of his death.

When further investigations were carried out on the unidentified man, these confirmed that he was Alexander Fallon, the person my automatic writing had identified as Alex!

Another project I was working on at this time involved me trying to cast new light on the Jack the Ripper murders that took place in the streets of Whitechapel during 1888.

I soon discovered that the name 'Jack the Ripper', which the police gave the unidentified murderer, has always been considered misleading. Far from ripping the flesh from his unfortunate victims, who were thought to number between five and seven homeless women, 'Jack' appeared to be an expert at slitting throats and mutilating bodies. In fact, his gruesome handiwork was so expertly done that many people thought he must have been a surgeon or a butcher.

Many theories have been aired about his identity since the 1880s, and some rumours have even suggested that 'Jack' was a member of our Royal Family. Despite all the ongoing investigations, however, his identity has remained a mystery, and I was hoping that I could shed some light on what had happened to those poor women in the gas-lit alleyways and fog-bound lanes of the East End of London.

During the filming, I met Paul, a 'Rippertologist', and once again I did some automatic writing. I was also shown a picture of Mary Jane Kelly, one of the murder victims, and that really spurred my psychic powers on. The first thing I picked up on was that there were far more than five murder victims, and that the first two victims had been black women who were killed not in the East End of London, but in America! The pull of the Britain/America connection was so strong, I really could not doubt it.

Included in the information that then came through in automatic writing were the names 'Florence' and 'Miller'.

Paul then told me that Florence was the name of the wife of one of the murder suspects, and that the mutilated body of Mary Jane Kelly had been found in Miller's Court (now named White's Row). I also saw numbers in my mind's eye, which proved to be the correct year for one of the murders.

The next piece of filming was in a cemetery, where Mary Jane Kelly was buried. Here I picked up some really strange vibes at the graveside. In my mind I saw a man dressed in a hat and long dark cloak walking into a small dark room. This image, which came and went in a second or two, was very chilling.

Having finished filming at the cemetery, we went to Whitechapel. Throughout the nineteenth century, this area was notorious for its slum housing and poor sanitary conditions. With a pub on almost every street corner, many of which were open all day, alcoholism became rife. The area has always been a home for immigrants from all over the world. The French Huguenots, who arrived in the seventeenth century, were followed by Eastern European Jews in the middle of the nineteenth century, then by Bangladeshi people after the Second World War. Today, Whitechapel is a very busy area that is still thronged with people of different cultures and nationalities.

Having arrived there, I had to overcome my intense desire just to wander and enjoy, and, trailed by the camera crew, I walked with Paul along a road to where one of the Ripper's victims had been murdered.

'When we get near to where we are going,' Paul said, 'I want you – *if you can* – to tell me the actual spot where the murder took place.'

It was a tall order!

'It's difficult sometimes,' I began, 'so many feet have passed through these streets since the murder that any vibes that were once present have become very watered down.'

Nevertheless, as we walked on, I found myself compelled to stop and look to the right of me where there was a parade of shops that had older-style Victorian buildings above them. Having arrived outside one of these, I suddenly felt myself freeze and I stood gazing up at the window.

'Why have you stopped here?' Paul asked.

'I just feel very drawn to this place,' I replied.

'Well . . . this is the building where the inquests were held for Jack the Ripper's victims.'

'I know,' I said quietly, 'because I have such a strong image in my mind of the Ripper himself being in this building. I can see him looking out of that window on to a massive crowd of people who have gathered below to wait for something like a verdict.'

It was creepy, but I knew instinctively that Jack had been there, ghoulishly watching – *enjoying* – the day's proceedings.

Paul, who was a very cautious, analytical guy and a some-what guarded 'Rippertologist', was not particularly impressed by what I had just picked up, but there was still hope for me! Alongside the building where I had stopped was a little alleyway, and I was now experiencing a strong urge to walk into this dark, dank pathway. It was a really sinister-looking place, and as I walked I felt that I was being transformed into a woman, who was constantly looking over her shoulder, convinced she was being followed.

'Well . . . let's face it,' Paul replied when I paused to tell him this, 'this is a dark, smelly, unsavoury alleyway, and it would be reasonable for your mind to play such tricks on you.'

'I don't know,' I retorted. 'All I know is that now I've reached the end of this alleyway, I want to go this way – in the direction of that footbridge.'

'OK,' Paul agreed.

Having crossed the footbridge, I found myself brought to a halt again outside another building. As I stood there, Paul said, 'Yes, this is the area where one of the victims was found. I was actually going to approach it from the other direction, but you led us this way.'

I noted that he was looking slightly more impressed, but he was not yet convinced by my psychic abilities.

'I'm going to walk around this building to see if I can sense what went on here,' I said.

It was possible to approach the tall Victorian building from three sides, but I immediately excluded two of these and responded to the draw of the other.

'I think the murder took place here,' I exclaimed. 'The poor woman was shoved against this wall. She tried to run – and I now feel I want to draw a line on the ground from where we are standing to about thirty feet away.'

Paul was not a man who was given to awarding Brownie points! 'No,' he said, 'you're wrong.' Then, pointing to a spot about fifteen feet away, he added, 'The murder actually took place there.'

'Well, I think you're wrong,' I replied gently. 'But even if you're right, Paul, I still think it's pretty good to get within fifteen feet of the spot where the murder took place. And for all you know, the attack could have started here before the victim was dragged fifteen feet to where her body was found.'

Despite all my doubts about watered down vibes, the experience of walking through the narrow lanes of Whitechapel was proving quite fruitful. On several occasions I felt myself transported back, via vivid flashbacks, to that grisly time in the 1880s.

'The house where Mary Jane Kelly's room once existed in Miller's Court has long since been pulled down, and there is now a warehouse erected on the site,' Paul explained. 'But we'll go there next.'

Having walked in the rain to the site, I kept wanting to get about ten feet further inside the building that was now erected there.

'That *is* strange,' Paul conceded, 'because the original houses were set back about ten feet from the road.'

I then sensed a maze of squalid-looking houses and alleyways, and I was able to describe one particular alleyway that I had a very clear image of in my mind's eye. I was also able to describe the doorway of the house where Mary Jane Kelly had lived, and where the stairs and her room had been positioned within it. I also knew instinctively that when she opened the door to her room, it hit against the side of a wooden cabinet. I knew exactly where her bed was placed in the room and I could see her body lying on it. As I stood at the foot of the bed, I knew there were two windows that let in two areas of light, and that something was etched on the wall.

When I mentioned this to Paul, he confirmed that after the Ripper had murdered Mary Jane in her room, he had etched some initials in blood on the wall. I also sensed that Jack had known this victim and that he was taking revenge for something that she knew about him or had done to him. I sensed that he was a tall, slim man, with a large black moustache, who wore a tall hat, a black cloak and carried a silver-topped cane. I had no sense of him being a member of the Royal Family. I also sensed that he had an accomplice, and I could feel this man, who acted as a lookout, peering through a cracked pane of glass in a window. The whole scene was very real to me – Jack the Ripper, the accomplice, Mary Jane, the bedroom and the etching on the wall.

During the last part of the filming, I was invited up to IPM's office where they had managed to trace one of the last descendants – a great-great-great granddaughter – of one of Jack the Ripper's victims. When I read for this woman, who had only learned that she was a descendant a few years ago, I described a man who had died seven years ago and was able to give her a very poignant message from him.

During the reading, I picked up on the name Kate or Kath, and I was able to tell the lady how Kate had felt and what she had known of the murderer. I subsequently learned that one of Jack's victim's was Catherine (Kate) Eddows. Born in Wolverhampton in 1848, she had travelled on foot to London with her family when she was just eight years old, and had died at the hands of the Ripper when she was forty-six while trying to earn some money for a bed for the night.

One of my all-time favourite messages came through during a demonstration, when I was standing in the centre of a room with columns, surrounded by about 120 people on all four sides of me. At first, when I began to speak, I thought I was describing my own Auntie Grace because the description I was giving was so like her.

'I have a lady here,' I announced. 'A beautiful, brassy-looking, very funny lady.'

The next moment, though, all thoughts of my auntie were dispelled and I went on to describe a woman who had dark, backcombed hair, and who wore spectacles and a great deal of make-up. She was a vibrant character with a great sense of humour, who had gorgeous legs and who was wearing high-heeled stiletto shoes. As I finished describing her, a hand went up.

'Do you know this person, darling?' I asked.

'Yes – yes I do,' the woman replied with total certainty.

'The lady I am seeing is definitely standing behind a bar, pulling a pint of beer,' I added.

'Oh yes, that's definitely her,' the woman exclaimed, thrilled. 'It's my auntie. She was a barmaid.'

'She's just said that you are so like her.'

'Yes,' she agreed. 'I'm a barmaid, too.'

'And she only ever wore high-heeled shoes? And she had a rather big bust?'

'Oh yes, that's her, she did.'

'Well, she has come this evening to give you all her love.'

When I finished the reading, I thanked the audience and brought the first half of the demonstration to an end. During the interval, the young lady came up to me and said, 'Those messages from my auntie were really amazing – *lovely* – but I wish she had mentioned that I've got cancer. When she said I was just like her, I thought she had realised that, just like her, I have cancer, and that tomorrow I'm going into hospital for a major operation. I do wish she had come back because she knew that.'

'I'm sorry, darling,' I said, 'maybe she did know and I just didn't get that part of her message.'

At the start of the second half, I began by describing a mother.

'I've got a mum here,' I announced, 'who's looking for her daughter and she's calling out the name Bet Lynch.'

At this, the hand of a girl, who was sitting next to the lady I was speaking to in the interval, shot up.

'Oh, that's my mum,' she called out confidently. 'She always said I looked like Bet Lynch and she – and everybody else now – always calls me Bet Lynch.'

'Your mum is telling me that somebody is wearing her earrings and, while she's doing that, she's also pointing to her tummy. So the person who's wearing her earrings has something wrong with her tummy. She's saying to me, "She'll be fine, darling, just fine".'

By now, the two women were both jumping up and down and calling out, and the woman I had spoken to during the interval was sobbing her heart out and saying, 'My friend made me put her mum's earrings on tonight, and that's where my cancer is, *in my tummy*. And she's now saying that I'm going to be OK.'

It was an extraordinary moment. Her auntie may not have communicated anything about the cancer, but her friend's mother had. I have learned, though, that there is never any point in wondering about the whys and wherefores of the ways in which the spirits communicate with us. All that mattered that day was that although the girl who was wearing the earrings had never met her friend's mother when she was alive, the woman had taken the trouble to come through to comfort her.

I loved both that first reading and the subsequent message that came through after the break. It was a really special occasion that seemed to run the whole gamut of emotions, from fun and humourous to serious and sombre, and it ended on a delightfully upbeat note that left the young woman feeling so much stronger and full of hope.

I could never have guessed when I first began this work that life could be so full of extraordinary events and momentous moments.

The truth is I enjoy *all* my work, but the most rewarding element remains one-to-one readings. The joy of helping people to be reunited, reconnected with their loved one has never palled. By way of contrast, I also love doing larger theatre demonstrations to 2,000 people or more. I know that many of the people who attend these come along thinking they will have a good laugh and then go to the pub afterwards. But if it is a good demonstration they leave in a very different frame of mind. Having witnessed people getting messages and seeing them crying with happiness or relief, or gasping when they are given the correct name from hundreds of thousands of possibilities, it gives them a jolt, shakes them up, plants a seed, and I can feel them thinking, 'Perhaps there *is* something in this after all.' Nothing, in my view, could be more satisfying!

Most of us go through life being shunted backwards and forwards in a routine, day-in-day-out kind of way, until something like a visit to a demonstration of the paranormal rocks our whole world.

'Damn!' we may exclaim. 'I thought I was safe in thinking "when we're dead, we're dead", and I was only living for today, but now I'm not so sure.'

In general, there is such a fear of death that many people feel as if the ground is mined beneath their feet, and they are so busy worrying about it that they do not appreciate the life they have! Some will do almost anything to cheat the great reaper; they will arrange for their bodies to be embalmed or packed in ice when they die, just in case they can be resuscitated and brought back to life one day. But 'Hey – what's the point?', I long to say to comfort and reassure them. 'The truth is that you *will* live again!'

I was just a child when I first came to believe that we cannot die, that life is eternal, and throughout all the intervening years when I have worked as a psychic medium, nothing has happened to change that belief. Death *truly* has no sting, and grave no victory!

Epilogue

I am a lucky man. I have been blessed with the ability to work in many different aspects of the paranormal, and I have wonderful spirit guides to help me with my mediumship, and with my psychic work. I am also sure, thanks to the spirits who use me, that my work brings closure for many people who have previously doubted that there is life after death, and who come to realise that life truly is eternal and that we will be born again.

As for those future lives, I think our spirit will be reborn into the kind of body and set of circumstances that our karma requires it to be reborn into. However many incarnations we may have experienced already, there may be many others still to come. I also believe, though, that there will come a time in our spiritual evolution when we will remain in the higher realms of truth, consciousness and bliss, without the need to take on a particular gender. The most beautiful spirit guides I have seen live in those realms and are androgynous.

In the house in which I now live, I no longer have a particular room that I set aside as a sanctuary. Instead I try to make the whole house a sanctuary. Often when I am home alone, I do not switch on the television, listen to music or read. I just light candles in the room and sit quietly by the fire. Candlelight and firelight create a very meditative, spiritual atmosphere, and I do not consider it at all fanciful to believe that the present flame stems from the original flame and therefore the same flame that lit up my past lives. The five elements – fire, air, ether, earth and water – are so essential to our well-being. We cannot always have the sound of water gushing around our homes, or a cooling breeze rippling through our hair, but we can have the element of fire present in a living flame.

Many religions, both in the East and West, make constant references to light – 'the light within us', 'the eternal flame', 'the spark of divinity' – and the suggestion is that each individual light will one day merge with the light of the Great Spirit. I certainly believe that each of us can be likened to a little candle in the world. I am aware that some people keep stubbing out their light, but there are also those among us who are happy to devote their lives to reigniting the eternal flame in others.

My only fear in life – and it is a cross I bear every day – is that I will not accomplish all that I want to accomplish before I come to the end of this particular embodiment. If this comes to pass and I do not get as much done as I should – or I do not do as well as I should – I will be very disappointed. But I am determined that this will not happen and that I will repay the blessings I have been given by being a good, clear channel for the spirits.

Perhaps the constant fear that I am not doing enough to earn the privilege of having been so blessed and to justify my present existence is a healthy one. Certainly it inspires me to work hard. In 2004 I am doing a tour of the UK, the US and South Africa, and when I am in the UK I will do readings as often as I can. I get so much pleasure from this work and the people I meet, and the more I do, the more people want me to do. I also enjoy my work in different parts of Europe, and I will continue to work there as often as I can.

All these activities help to counteract my fear that I am not doing enough. I am very aware, for example, that I could have been born into a country that was torn apart by war, or a place where drought and famine meant that I had only sufficient energy to survive. But I have been blessed by being born into the UK and with having good parents, a loving sister, great friends and a comfortable home of my own. All this means that I have energy left over from the nitty-gritty of everyday life, and the freedom to look beyond the Now. Having a roof over one's head, food in one's belly and clothes on one's back is a phenomenal privilege. I realise that some people who have all these things take them for granted and still want more. But that's OK. We have all been there at one time or another, and with the right influences, those who are there now will start to count their blessings and begin to consider what they can do with their lives other than looking for more of the same – bigger houses, better cars and the accumulation of yet more personal wealth.

Every demonstration and reading I do, I am aware that there is the potential for the spirits to use me to change people's lives and beliefs for the better. Those around me get very frustrated when I come off stage and say to them, 'Oh God, I should have done better. I should have got that name. I should . . .'

'Come on,' they reply. 'You did your best, Tony. Whatever you think, we *know* you touched somebody's life tonight.'

I am sure, thanks to my spirit guides, that that is true, but I want to do even better! My one comfort is that while I feel so driven, my ego will never get the better of me and I will never become complacent. Over the years many a gifted medium has made the mistake of believing that the messenger is more important than the message or the spirits from which it comes, and I do not want to fall into that trap. I may not become as good or as useful as I want to be in this lifetime, but maybe that's no bad thing. Maybe that will keep my ego under control and my feet firmly on the ground.

'God works in mysterious ways his wonders to perform . . .' goes the saying. And as I have discovered, these 'wonders' often come about in very ordinary moments and in seemingly mundane ways. When I was seventeen, I read Shirley MacLaine's autobiography *Out On a Limb*, and the life story of this brilliant actress instantly transported me to 'other worldly' things. It was a life-changing read.

When I first picked up the book, I thought I was just reading it for pleasure, but it proved to be so wonderful that it *really* inspired me and I have never forgotten it. What became obvious when reading it was that Shirley MacLaine, unlikely though this may sound, was a superb New Age guru who spoke good, uplifting sense. Among other things, she revealed a great deal about her own inner struggle to make contact with her spiritual self, and told us how, through discovering Buddhism and making a visit to a mountain top in Peru, her spiritual life had started to unfold. At that age, when my interest in the paranormal was just beginning to take root and my friends could have been forgiven for thinking I was a bit strange, this book was very important to me.

Its title, *Out On a Limb*, was based on the old saying: 'Sometimes to get to the fruit of the tree, you have to go out on a limb.' I have never forgotten this quote. It had a major impact on my life then and I have lived by it ever since.

In 2003, when I was thinking of giving up my wedding planning work to go for my spiritual work full-time, I opened myself to the spirit world and asked the spirits what I should do.

'Sometimes to get to the fruit of the tree,' the answer bounced back, 'you have to go out on a limb.'

I have decided that when my time comes, this will be my epitaph and I will arrange for the saying to be etched on my tombstone. It is something I truly feel I have spent this life doing, and I have never regretted it – not for one minute of any one day.

HODDER
MOBIUS

**Transform your life
with Hodder Mobius**

For the latest information on the best in
Spirituality, Self-Help,
Health & Wellbeing and Parenting,

visit our website
www.hoddermobius.com